Reflections on
the Art of Living

for Joseph
    for the young Parzival
        for the Imperishable

Reflections on
the Art of Living

A
Joseph
Campbell
Companion

Selected and Edited by
Diane K. Osbon

HarperPerennial
A Division of HarperCollinsPublishers

A hardcover edition of this work was published in 1991 by
HarperCollins Publishers.

See page 309 for permissions.

Acknowledgments
Grateful acknowledgments to The Joseph Campbell Foundation,
to Paul B. Herbert of Dolphin Tapes, to the many other holders of
copyrights for their generous permissions, to Carol Cohen, Burton
Fine, and Timothy Seldes for their professionalism, to friends and
scholars Bette Andresen, Elizabeth Borges, Julie Borges, Robert E.
Cook, Ralph Adam Fine, Carol Gutenkunst, Clifford Charles
Keck, Michael Lemle, Clair Miller, Clayton Osbon, and Barbara
Wall—for their time and support.

A special thanks to Jean Erdman Campbell whose love,
encouragement, and wisdom made this possible.

D.K.O.

Frontispiece drawing by Robin Larsen

FIRST HARPERPERENNIAL EDITION

ISBN 0-06-092617-1

02 03 04 MAC/RRD 24

Contents

Reflections on
the Art of Living

Introduction

"There is no place in this new kind of physics both for the field and matter, for the field is the only reality."
—Albert Einstein[1]

It is on this very point that Eastern mysticism and Western science meet. *Tat tvam asi*, "thou art that," is the bottom line of Joseph Campbell's philosophy. There is no matter; everything is the field. The separations and limitations are in our own minds.

To separate oneself or one's group—to say, "Oh, no, *we* are different"—is to set oneself against wholeness. To separate ourselves from the whole is to cut our options and erect the walls of our own prison. When we create duality in our thoughts and lives, we have created opposition.

In an intimate seminar of ten people gathered at Esalen Institute for one month in 1983, Joseph Campbell processed each one's life with professional sensitivity. Our total immersion in the mythic realm resulted in such a cohesiveness and intensity that the director of Esalen asked Joseph if he could sit in on a session. Without missing a beat, Joseph's response was: "That would not be appropriate." A sacred circle had been created, within which it was safe to plumb one's depth, express doubts, and trade stories of magic and rapture. The seminar ended with Joseph saying that he was certain that it had been a destiny gathering. The real humanity of this elegant power field of a man was his gift to us. Like Parzival, *"he was not an angel or a saint, but a living questing man of deeds, gifted with the*

7

paired virtues of courage and compassion, to which was added loyalty. And it was through his steadfastness in these—not supernatural grace—that he won, at last, to the Grail."[2]

The inspiration for this book came from times spent with Joseph. The text has been taken in large part from that month-long, intensive seminar at Esalen. Appropriate quotes from his books, set in italics, have been added for balance and radiance. The aphorisms of the opening section (*In the Field*), as well as those throughout the rest of the book, are favorite expressions of his, recorded in my journals over the years in his company. The rest of the book is divided into three parts, which correspond to three levels, or stages, of consciousness.

The first part (*Living in the World*) deals primarily with the pelvic energy centers—survival, sex, and power. Here Joseph shares his thoughts regarding money, the opposite sex, patterns of aging, death, marriage, war, procreation, ritual, etc. He teaches that doing what someone else wants us to do is slave morality and a path to disease and disintegration of the spirit and body. He advises us to listen when someone is speaking, not to the words, but to *what* is talking—it is often pride, malice, or ignorance. For example, when someone tells us that we are selfish, it is often because we are not doing what *they* want us to do. As we restrict our options, we restrict our world view and, with sufficient restriction, we can become the "world's policeman," who zealously guards to see that others do not break out of the box that he has built for himself.

The next stage (*Coming into Awareness*) opens us to the possibilities of our own deep love and truths. As we love ourselves, we move toward our own bliss, by which Joseph Campbell meant our highest enthusiasm. The word *entheos* means "god-filled." Moving toward that which fills us with the godhood, that place where time is not, is all we need to do to change the world

8

around us. Then do we, naturally and without effort, love others and allow them to move beyond their self-imposed limitations, and in their own ways. The goal is to evolve to that place where the energy that had been projected outward to correct the world is turned around to correct oneself—to get on our own track and to dance, in balance, between the worlds.

As we evolve into the final level (*Living in the Sacred*), we see that we can choose to lift the veil of illusion (*maya*) to reveal the Kingdom of the Father that is spread upon the earth, for we are the maya makers. It is then that the rhythm of the spheres moves through us and the Universal heartbeat is our own.

Joseph taught me to see beyond the symbols to the riches they represent. Those who cannot see beyond the symbols, he remarked, are "like diners going into a restaurant and eating the menu," rather than the meal it describes. There is a good deal of menu eating in the world, and the result is a feeling of emptiness and an impoverishment of spirit.

Being in his presence, one realized that everything he focused on, in nature or in conversation, was a spark that illuminated another volume in the vast library of his mind, a bottomless spring of riches and sustenance. His open countenance revealed that he was his own greatest resource for wonder and magic. It is not surprising that his first deep love was the American Indian, to whom every part of nature is sacred.

Living in that rapture *is* health. And following your bliss, understood as Joseph meant it, is not self-indulgent, but vital: your whole physical system knows that this is the way to be alive in this world and the way to give to the world the very best that you have to offer. There *is* a track just waiting there for each of us, and once on it, doors will open that were not open before and would not open for anyone else. Everything does start clicking along and, yes, even Mother Nature herself supports the journey.

I have found that you do have only to take that one step toward the gods and they will then take ten steps toward you. That step, the heroic first step of the journey, is out of, or over the edge of, your boundaries, and it often must be taken before you know that you will be supported. The hero's journey has been compared to a birth: it starts with being warm and snug in a safe place; then comes a signal, growing more insistent, that it is time to leave. To stay beyond your time is to putrefy. Without the blood and tearing and pain, there is no new life.

"What is the meaning of life?" Joseph was often asked, and he would respond, "There is no meaning. We bring the meaning to it." Like Carl Jung, he saw the approach of old age, not as a mere diminution of life, but as a time of blooming. If we have filled up the beaker of life and allowed to catch fire everything that needs to be consumed, then the quiet of old age is welcome. If too much life remains unlived, we approach the threshold of old age with unsatisfied demands that turn our glances backward. As Jung said, "An old man who cannot bid farewell to life appears as feeble and sickly as a young man who is unable to embrace it."[3]

Joseph taught that we can choose to live in rapture, that it is not "out there" in some other place or person, that we don't have to go somewhere or have something or someone. "It is *here*. It is *here*. It is *here*." A shift in consciousness is all it takes.

"Unless you become as little children, you shall not enter the Kingdom of Heaven."[4]

As children, we knew when to be still and watchful, so as to bring just the right people and creatures toward us. It was easy, and the magic was everywhere. We lose that childhood magic in the world of masks, but we are meant to return to the child. As Joseph put it, "The lion of self-discovery is meant to kill that dragon whose every scale reads 'Thou Shalt.'"

After working with Joseph, honoring the birth of the spiritual and creative child within myself sanctifies the Christmas season now. The lighted tree is the wish-fulfilling tree, the World Tree, the *axis mundi*. And as the tender plants push up and reach for the heavens, I celebrate Easter as release and renewal—leaving the Earth Mother to go to the Father Spirit. Every egg now is the Cosmic Egg, the unshelled chick symbolic of the birth of the spirit; each rabbit is a symbol of the moon's cycle of loss and gain—ever changing, ever the same.

An old Apache storyteller reminds us: *"The plants, rocks, fire, water, all are alive. They watch us and see our needs. They see when we have nothing to protect us, and it is then that they reveal themselves and speak to us."*[5]

I remember the quote Joseph loved from the Gnostic Gospel of St. Thomas: *"Cleave a piece of wood, I am there. Lift up the stone, you will find me there."*

"Why are there trees I never walk under but large and melodious thoughts descend upon me?" Walt Whitman asks. *"I think they hang there Winter and Summer on those trees and only drop fruit as I pass"*[6]

The people of Findhorn, Scotland, believe that the consciousness of trees goes *beyond the sawmill,* that they are aware of the homes into which they are made and the people they shelter...

this home

this chair

this page

It is here   It is here   It is here

—D.K.O.

11

In the Field

THE privilege of a lifetime is being who you are.

What you have to do,
you do with play.

Life is without meaning.
You bring the meaning to it.

The meaning of life is
whatever you ascribe it to be.

Being alive is the meaning.

The warrior's approach
is to say "yes" to life:
"yea" to it all.

Participate joyfully
in the sorrows of the world.

We cannot cure the world of sorrows,
but we can choose to live in joy.

When we talk about
settling the world's problems,
we're barking up the wrong tree.

The world is perfect. It's a mess.
It has always been a mess.

We are not going to change it.

Our job is to straighten out
our own lives.

We must be willing to get rid of
the life we've planned, so as to have
the life that is waiting for us.

The old skin has to be shed
before the new one can come.

If we fix on the old, we get stuck.
When we hang onto any form,
we are in danger of putrefaction.

Hell is life drying up.

The Hoarder,
the one in us that wants to keep,
to hold on, must be killed.

If we are hanging onto the form now,
we're not going to have the form next.

You can't make an omelet
without breaking eggs.

Destruction before creation.

Out of perfection
nothing can be made.

Every process involves
breaking something up.

The earth must be broken
to bring forth life.

If the seed does not die,
there is no plant.

Bread results
from the death of wheat.

Life lives on lives.

Our own life
lives on the acts
of other people.

If you are lifeworthy,
you can take it.

What we are really living for
is the experience of life,
both the pain and the pleasure.

The world is a match for us.
We are a match for the world.

Opportunities
to find deeper powers
within ourselves
come when life
seems most challenging.

Negativism
to the pain and ferocity of life
is negativism to life.

We are not there
until we can say
"yea" to it all.

To take a righteous attitude
toward anything is to denigrate it.

Awe is what moves us forward.

As you proceed through life,
following your own path,
birds will shit on you.
Don't bother to brush it off.

Getting a comedic view
of your situation
gives you spiritual distance.
Having a sense of humor saves you.

Eternity
is a dimension
of here and now.

The divine lives within you.

Live from your own center.

Your real duty
is to go away from the community
to find your bliss.

The society is the enemy
when it imposes its structures
on the individual.

On the dragon there are many scales.
Everyone of them says "Thou Shalt."

Kill the dragon "Thou Shalt."

When one has killed that dragon,
one has become The Child.

Breaking out
is following your bliss pattern,
quitting the old place,
starting your hero journey,
following your bliss.

You throw off yesterday
as the snake sheds its skin.

Follow your bliss.

The heroic life is living the *individual*
adventure.

There is no security
in following the call to adventure.

Nothing is exciting
if you know
what the outcome is going to be.

To refuse the call
means stagnation.

What you don't experience positively
you will experience negatively.

You enter the forest
at the darkest point,
where there is no path.

Where there is a way or path,
it is someone else's path.

You are not on your own path.

If you follow someone else's way,
you are not going to realize
your potential.

The goal of the hero trip
down to the jewel point
is to find those levels in the psyche
that open, open, open,
and finally open to the mystery
of your Self being
Buddha consciousness
or the Christ.

That's the journey.

It is all about finding
that still point in your mind
where commitment drops away.

It is by going down into the abyss
that we recover the treasures of life.

Where you stumble,
there lies your treasure.

The very cave you are afraid to enter
turns out to be the source of
what you are looking for.
The damned thing in the cave
that was so dreaded
has become the center.

You find the jewel,
and it draws you off.

In loving the spiritual,
you cannot despise the earthly.

The purpose of the journey
is compassion.

When you have come past
the pairs of opposites,
you have reached compassion.

The goal is to bring the jewel
back to the world,
to join the two things together.

The separateness
apparent in the world
is secondary.

Beyond that world of opposites
is an unseen, but experienced,
unity and identity in us all.

Today, the planet is
the only proper "in group."

You must return
with the bliss
and integrate it.

The return is seeing
the radiance everywhere.

Sri Ramakrishna said:
"Do not seek illumination
unless you seek it
as a man whose hair is on fire
seeks a pond."

If you want the whole thing,
the gods will give it to you.
But you must be ready for it.

The goal is to live
with godlike composure
on the full rush of energy,
like Dionysus riding the leopard,
without being torn to pieces.

A bit of advice
given to a young Native American
at the time of his initiation:

"As you go the way of life,
you will see a great chasm.

Jump.

It is not as wide as you think."

Living
in the World

GOD had a garden, and he needed a gardener, so he created Adam. Adam was bored. He was doing the job, but it was no fun. God saw that he needed entertainment, and so he created the animals to entertain him. All Adam could think of to do with the animals was to give them names.

Then God said, "Well, here goes." So he put Adam to sleep and pulled Eve out of his rib—as Joyce said, she was "the cutletsized consort." Then the trouble started and we were in the game.

> Male and female, life and death,
> good and evil: problems of opposites.

The trouble that began was the discovery of duality. That was the Fall. There was no real recognition of duality before this. How did duality take place in this garden? There were two trees that were forbidden trees. "You can eat the fruit of any tree in the place but not of this or of that one." Tree number one was the tree of the knowledge of good and evil, of duality. Tree number two was the tree of the knowledge of eternal life.

The serpent—who represents lunar consciousness and life in the field of time, where there are pairs of opposites—saw Eve and thought she must be bored, as most wives are when their husbands are working all the time. When that happens, there's always a friend that appears, and this one was a little serpent.

The serpent said: "Look there's an interesting thing about this tree. Don't mind that old buzzard—have a taste and you will really know something." Well, she had a taste, and when Adam came along, she said, "Look, this is okay."

So, he had a taste, and then God, who walked in the cool of the evening in the Garden, saw the pair of them wearing fig leaves, and he said, "What's this? You've got leaves on."

> The female activates the male;
> then he is the action,
> and she has to take the results.

They told God what happened, and that ran the usual way: the man blamed the woman, and the woman blamed the snake. God then cursed the lot of them in increasing degrees. Man got it fairly easy: all he had to do was to work and sweat. The woman had to bring forth children in pain, and the serpent had to crawl on his belly for the rest of his life. God kicked them out of the Garden and put at the gate two cherubim, door guardians, with a flaming sword between them. And that's the explanation of why we're out here in the cold and not in the Garden.

> Christianity and Judaism
> are religions of exile:
> Man was thrown out of the Garden.

It seems impossible today, but people actually believed all that until as recently as half a century or so ago: clergymen, philosophers, government officers and all. Today we know— and know right well—that there never was anything of the

*kind: no Garden of Eden anywhere on this earth, no time
when the serpent could talk, no prehistoric "Fall," no exclusion from the Garden, no universal Flood, no Noah's Ark.
The entire history on which our leading Occidental religions
have been founded is an anthology of fictions. But these are
fictions of a type that have had—curiously enough—a
universal vogue as the founding legends of other religions,
too. Their counterparts have turned up everywhere—and yet,
there never was such a garden, serpent, tree, or deluge.*[7]

The serpent
was the wise one in the Garden.
Adam and Eve
got thrown into the field of time.

*"...in the beginning this universe was but the Self in
the form of a man. He looked around and saw nothing but
himself....*

*"He was just as large as a man and a woman embracing.
This Self then divided himself in two parts; and with that,
there were a master and mistress.—Therefore this body, by
itself, as the sage Yajnavalkya declares, is like half of a split
pea. And that is why, indeed, this space is filled by a
woman.—He united with her, and from that mankind
arose....*

*"She became a cow, he a bull and united with her; and
from that cattle arose. She became a mare, he a stallion; she
an ass, he a donkey and united with her; and from that
solid-hoofed animals arose. She became a goat, he a buck;
she became a sheep, he a ram and united with her; and from
that goats and sheep arose.—Thus he poured forth all
pairing things, down to the ants."* —Brihadaranyaka
Upanishad[8]

Marriage is reconstruction
of the androgyne.

31

If you marry only for the love affair,
that will not last.

You must also marry on another level
to reconstruct the androgyne,
to make the perfect whole,
male and female.

...*consider the allegory in Plato's* Symposium, *where it
is said by Aristophanes—playfully, yet in the form of the
same myth—that the earliest human beings were "round and
had four hands and four feet, back and sides forming a circle,
one head with two faces looking opposite ways, set on a
round neck and precisely alike; also four ears, two privy
members, and the remainders to correspond." According to this
Platonic version of the great theme, these original creatures
were of three kinds: male-male, male-female, and female-
female. They were immensely powerful; and since the gods
were in fear of their strength, Zeus decided to cut them in
two, like apples halved for pickling.... "After the division
the two parts of man, each desiring his other half, came together, and threw their arms about one another eager to grow
into one, and would have perished from hunger without ever
making an effort, because they did not like to do anything
apart... : so ancient is the desire of one another which is im-
planted in us, reuniting our original nature, making one of
two and healing the state of man. Each of us when separated
is but the indenture of a man, having one side only like a flat
fish, and he is always looking for his other half.*[9]

When seeking your partner,
if your intuition is a virtuous one,
you will find him or her. If not,
you'll keep finding the wrong person.

How does one talk about whether or not there is a destiny between couples? I feel it, but I don't believe it. In my case, at Sarah Lawrence College I was teaching all these beautiful girls, and there were certain classes when I'd feel a little hopped up. It took me six months to locate the one who was responsible for this, and when I did, I knew I was gone.

When I first saw the woman who is now my wife, I felt like that and didn't know it. She was in the class, and I was hopped up—who the hell is doing this? Then I finally located who she was, and there was a whole constellating of relationship that I didn't let her know about until I gave the mildest sign: she was about to leave school, so I gave her a book: Spengler's *Decline of the West*. It was a little present, but a loaded one.

There was something behind that projection of mine. Why does this projection come out of me instead of someone else? Because it's based upon my deep life experiences, and that's where one's destiny is. It is structured by your own life. It is my life that put the projection that way—experiences that I've had of the female, even in my infancy.

So that's what destiny is: simply the fulfillment of the potentialities of the energies in your own system. The energies are committed in a certain way, and that commitment out there is coming toward you.

The projection-making factor [in the male] is the anima, or rather the unconscious as represented by the anima. Whenever she appears, in dreams, visions, and fantasies, she takes on personified form, thus demonstrating that the factor she embodies possesses all the outstanding characteristics of a feminine being. She is not an invention of the conscious, but a spontaneous product of the unconscious. Nor is she a substi tute figure for the mother. On the contrary, there is every likelihood that the numinous qualities which make the mother-image so dangerously powerful derive from the collective archetype of the anima, which is incarnated anew in every male child. —Jung [10]

> The woman's body
> is the first world to the newborn.
> The child's projections of *anima*
> will be of her from then on.

Just as the mother seems to be the first carrier of the projection-making factor for the son, so is the father for the daughter....Woman is compensated by a masculine element and therefore her unconscious has, so to speak, a masculine imprint. This results in a considerable psychological difference between men and women, and accordingly I have called the projection-making factor in women the animus, which means mind or spirit....when anima and animus meet, the animus draws his sword of power, and the anima ejects her poison of illusion and seduction. The outcome need not always be negative, since the two are equally likely to fall in love (a special instance of love at first sight). —Jung[11]

> You know about your anima or animus
> by your response to the opposite sex.

There's a fundamental image in the old Babylonian mythology of the God Marduk, the great sun god, the shaper and creator of the world. What does he create the world out of? His grandmother, Tiamat, who comes as a monster, and he carves her up.

She would have cut herself up anyhow, but she lets him become the agent of this deed, because one has to have that kind of confidence in action out there in order that the world can live. So, this is a generous woman, who lets the little boy think he is doing the job, when she could have done it herself.

That's the way the animus is: it is a projection of something the female could do but instead allows the male to do for her. Though not half so vital a presence, he is a machine with a body that's specialized, so he can do these things. The realization that the power is within you is one thing; but to realize that the action implied by that power is more adequately rendered by the male than by you as a female is to recognize relationship.

When a woman realizes that the power is within her, then the man emerges as an individual, rather than just being an example of what she thinks she needs. On the male side, when a man looks at a woman and sees only somebody to go to bed with, he is seeing her in relation to a fulfillment of some need of his own and not as a woman at all. It's like looking at cows and thinking only of roast beef.

> Falling in love is nature coming in.
> It starts with being carried off
> by the opposite sex.

It is amazing, but our theologians still are writing of agape *and* eros *and their radical opposition, as though these two were the final terms of the principle of "love": the former, "charity," godly and spiritual, being "of men toward each other in a community," and the latter, "lust," natural and fleshly, being "the urge, desire and delight of sex."*[12] *Nobody in a pulpit seems ever to have heard of* amor *as a third, selective, discriminating principle in contrast to the other two. For* amor *is neither of the right-hand path (the sublimating spirit, the mind and the community of man), nor of the indiscriminate left (the spontaneity of nature, the mutual incitement of the phallus and the womb), but is the path directly before one, of the eyes and their message to the heart.*

There is a poem to this point by a great troubadour (perhaps the greatest of all), Guiraut de Borneilh...:

> *So, through the eyes love attains the heart:*
> *For the eyes are the scouts of the heart,*
> *And the eyes go reconnoitering*
> *For what it would please the heart to possess.*
> *And when they are in full accord*
> *And firm, all three, in the one resolve,*
> *At that time, perfect love is born*
> *From what the eyes have made welcome to the heart.*
> *Not otherwise can love either be born or have*
>   *commencement*
> *Then by this birth and commencement moved by*
>   *inclination*
>
> *By the grace and by command*
> *Of these three, and from their pleasure,*
> *Love is born, who with fair hope*
> *Goes comforting her friends.*

For as all true lovers
Know, love is perfect kindness,
Which is born—there is no doubt—from the heart
    and eyes.
The eyes make it blossom; the heart matures it:
Love, which is the fruit of their very seed.[13]

> Troubadour love was born
> with the meeting of the eyes.
> The eyes are the scouts of love.
> If it is a gentle heart, love is born.

At the moment of the wakening to love, an object,
apparently without, "passes [in the words of Joyce] into the
soul forever....And the soul leaps at the call. To live, to err,
to fall, to triumph, to recreate life out of life!"[14]

> Love is not only a life experience,
> but also a mystical experience.
> In courtly love, the pain of love,
> the impossibility of fulfillment,
> was considered the essence of life.

For when a heart insists on its destiny, resisting the gen-
eral blandishment, then the agony is great; so too the danger.
Forces, however, will have been set in motion beyond the
reckoning of the senses. Sequences of events from the corners
of the world will draw gradually together, and miracles of
coincidence bring the inevitable to pass.[15]

> The distance of your love
> is the distance of your life.
>
> Love is exactly as strong as life.

The loss of a love and the pain of a broken relationship is an overload of projection. That's all it is. In youth, your whole life is this wonderful dream that *"This is It"*: this relationship is the fulfillment of my fantasy and I can't imagine life otherwise. No argument can quell this feeling of total projection, of everything in the other one. I guess we can all recall an episode of an adolescent relationship that seemed to be the all-in-all and then went to pieces for some reason.

When a relationship breaks off, it takes a person a little while to settle and find a new commitment. It's after the breakoff, when there is no new commitment and life has been divested of all of its potentials, that this painful reaction takes place. For some people this is a dangerous period.

The psyche knows how to heal, but it hurts. Sometimes the healing hurts more than the initial injury, but if you can survive it, you'll be stronger, because you've found a larger base. Every commitment is a narrowing, and when that commitment fails, you have to get back to a larger base and have the strength to hold to it.

Nietzsche was the one who did the job for me. At a certain moment in his life, the idea came to him of what he called "the love of your fate." Whatever your fate is, whatever the hell happens, you say, *"This is what I need."* It may look like a wreck, but go at it as though it were an opportunity, a challenge. If you bring love to that moment—not discouragement—you will find the strength is there. Any disaster you can survive is an improvement in your character, your stature, and your life. What a privilege! This is when the spontaneity of your own nature will have a chance to flow.

Then, when looking back at your life, you will see that the moments which seemed to be great failures

followed by wreckage were the incidents that shaped
the life you have now. You'll see that this is really true.
Nothing can happen to you that is not positive. Even
though it looks and feels at the moment like a negative
crisis, it is not. The crisis throws you back, and when
you are required to exhibit strength, it comes.

> The dark night of the soul
> comes just before revelation.
>
> When everything is lost,
> and all seems darkness,
> then comes the new life
> and all that is needed.

Jean and I have been married for forty-six years, and we have a kind of back and forth of feelings and intelligences, so that we've experienced "the one that is two and the two that are one." We do not have to theorize about it, we know what the hell it means. It's what Goethe calls the "Golden Wedding," and it is beautiful when that feeling becomes a fact in your life.

> Mythology helps you to identify
> the mysteries of the energies
> pouring through you.
>
> Therein lies your eternity.

It is nice to know enough about mythology to realize how beautiful such an experience can be. A lot of people could have the experience and not know they had it. One of the wonderful things about these age-old realizations that are constellated in the mythic images is that they let you know what it is you are experiencing.

> Mythology is an organization of images
> metaphoric of experience, action, and
> fulfillment of the human spirit
> in the field of a given culture at a given time.

The goal of the Golden Wedding is implicit in the first moment of a relationship. Old age is implicit in the generation of a child: the child's old age is there waiting. Similarly, the older you get, the more you realize that you are still a kid, and your early experiences are the ones that are now just opening out. It is one system all the time.

This is one of the big themes in James Joyce's *Finnegans Wake*. He has this image of the heroine, Anna Livia Plurabelle, as being the personification of the River Liffey that flows through Dublin.

The River Liffey rises in the hills south of Dublin as a little girl, those dancing little rivulets that are going to form the river. Then it flows north to a lovely suburban area, where you have the mother with her family: the mid-point of life. The river is the same river. Then it turns and runs through Dublin and becomes an old, dirty, city river, carrying all the rubbish of the city back to the ocean, the Father Ocean. The sun then brings the vapor up to the cloud, and it's now a little cloud in the Mother Womb of the blue sky. It floats over the hill and discharges the rain on the mountains.

> The first half of life
> we serve society—engagement.
> The second half of life
> we turn inward—disengagement.

She is the same person, the same river, all the time. Joyce makes it so you can feel the old woman in the little girl and the little girl in the old woman. It's marvelous. And it's the way you actually feel as you get older, if you are paying attention to the experiences you're having inside.

You know, they say that old people can't remember what happened yesterday, but they can remember with great vividness what happened fifty years ago. This is really true. In old age, you are relaxed from the immediate occasion of the day's summons, and you're sinking down into your memory system, which is as alive as can be. Moments with your parents that were crisis moments are right there with you. They become

41

important. They're determinate moments that help illuminate what the relationship was.

Sometimes when I look back, I think, "Son of a gun, you missed everything." It's funny how, at a certain age, all I could see were the negatives in the way I lived: I missed it that time, or another time I was a stupid boob. Now, I try not to think about it. I'm wanting to get to heaven, where they tell me that you don't remember all those things.

> In the age of decrepitude,
> you look back over your life
> with gratitude,
> and forward to death
> as a return home.

When Dante passed out of Purgatory, he drank at the river where all of his sins were wiped out of his memory. The first river from which he'd drunk forgave all of his sins, but that wasn't good enough, because then he still had to forget them.

In Hinduism, the religion of the God Vishnu is that of love. In the Vishnu way of analyzing love, there are five degrees of love and a model that represents each of these different stages. The whole discipline of seeking and achieving illumination can be conducted from the energy of this channel.

The first degree of love, that of servant to master, is a low degree of love: "Oh Lord, you are the master. I am the servant. Tell me what I am to do, and I shall do it." This is the way of the religion of law, where there are a lot of commands—ten commandments, a thousand commandments, a hundred and ten thousand commandments. It is a religion of fear. You have not awakened to the divine presence. It's out there, and you are here. This way is principally for people who have not had much time to devote themselves either to religious thinking or to love.

The model that represents this first stage is that of the little monkey king, Hanuman, who is the servant of Rama. I don't know whether there is a specific example of this stage in the Christian tradition, but there doesn't have to be, because the Christian tradition is nothing else for most people: obeying ten commandments here, ten commandments there.

Degree number two, the relationship of friend to friend, is the awakening of what *we* would call love. Here, one thinks of one's friend more than in the first situation. The model of this second stage of love, friend for friend, would be that of the apostles to Jesus, or of anyone who really is a lover of anything or anybody.

Sri Ramakrishna, a wonderful Hindu saint of the last century, once asked a woman who said she did not love God, "Is there nothing in the world that you do love?" And she answered, "I love my little nephew."

"Well then," he replied, "There He is. Your service is there." Whenever there is an experience of love as a spontaneous act, rather than as the following of a command, you have moved out of stage one and into stage two.

This is worth thinking about. How much religious service reaches that level? I'd say very little. Yet this is how it ought to be. Religious experience is greatly lowered when it's only a fulfillment of laws and commands, and you are but a willing or non-willing person doing or not doing as you are told. When it comes to a spontaneous relationship of love, you're in another category.

The third order of love is that of parent for child. It is a more intimate and intense affair than that of friend to friend. The image of this third order of love in the Christian system is the Christmas crib, in which the babe represents the coming to us of the Christ in our own hearts. This is symbolic of the awakening in your heart of the realization that the divine power is within you. It's the dawn of the true religious life. You are fostering the spiritual child within yourself. The model for this stage in the Hindu tradition is the love of the Gopis for the little boy Krishna, the naughty butter thief.

There's one very amusing Krishna episode, in which his foster mother is told that her little boy is outside eating mud. She goes out to clean the mud out of his mouth, and when he opens his mouth, he reveals to her all the heavens and hells and gods and demons in himself. She is , of course, stunned by this display, and her relationship to him would be pretty well damaged from then on if she remembered it, so he very kindly erases it from her memory. How we know that this event happened—since she was the only one who had the experience and then she forgot it—I do not know. But that's the way religious things are.

The fourth level of love is that of spouse to spouse, and here there is the business of the androgyne, of identification with the Other. You have found the god in your heart, and now the god is found in this intimate and most enduring kind of relationship. That's why marriage is regarded, in such traditions, as a permanent affair. There is only one chance to have this type of experience. Nuns wear a wedding ring, because they are brides of Christ. Their relationship is to this invisible spouse, which, on the spiritual level, is good enough.

Then we come to the highest order of love, the fifth, and that is compulsive, uncontrollable, illicit love, where there is nothing but love and you are totally ripped out of yourself in relation to God. You are *le fou*, the crazed one who's gone mad with love.

> In courtly love,
> the man goes crazy, not the woman.
> When the man's been moved like this,
> he is capable of incredible feats,
> but he's on a narrow path.
>
> When you follow your passion,
> society's help is gone.
> You must be very careful.
> You're completely on your own.

In marriage, one is still harmoniously related to society and to the neighborhood, but with this fifth stage of love, everything except love drops away, and there is just a one-pointed attachment to the other. All else is forgotten, and nothing else matters. I am sure some of you have had this experience. If you haven't, it's too bad.

In this little scale that the Hindus give—first servant to master; second, friend to friend; third, parent to child; fourth, spouse to spouse; and then fifth, just this total love—one is always in danger of over-valuing the sheer love experience. You feel that you are losing something if you pull the experience down, but you have got to pull it down. All you have to do, really, is know what the possible relationship can be.

If you're already married and this rapturous experience happens, then you're not going to have a marriage, because you've got to have some other kind of relationship to the person. The way to pull down the sheer love experience is to take very deep pleasure of some kind in the concrete aspects of the relationship that you are establishing. Sheer rapture has no relationship to life, but there *are* relationships in life which also have value. Begin to cultivate those, and this total rapture can be pulled down and not lost. It's not necessarily lost. And this is the trick in marriage.

There are lots of joyful experiences in marriage that have nothing to do with total rapture, but these experiences absorb that energy system and make it possible for one to stay married and not think it's only about taking out the garbage. Anyone who gets married is going to have problems with daily chores, because the problem of a household is on you whether you are a male or a female. But you can make wonderful little ritual experiences out of the things that have to be done, and life can ride beautifully on these events. I think it is a failure to accept the tangibilities of two people living together that makes marriages break up.

> Marriage is not a love affair,
> it's an ordeal.

It is a religious exercise, a sacrament,
the grace of participating in another life.

There is another kind of breakup that takes place
late in marriage, and this one just baffles me: people
who break up when the kids are out of the house and
launched. I have seen this happen in five or six cases to
people whom I never would have thought would have
had that happen. They are well on in their fifties, they
have been living together, they've brought up a family
together, had life together, and it goes to pot. The only
thing holding them together had been the children.

This is the failure of what I called the alchemical
marriage. They have had a biological marriage, but
there has been no realization of the interlocking of the
psyches and the mutual education that comes out of
that acquiescence and relationship. It's a damned shame
that there has been no preliminary notion of what the
possibilities are of that second half of life.

If you go into marriage with a program,
you will find that it won't work.

Successful marriage
is leading innovative lives together,
being open, non-programmed.
It's a free fall: how you handle
each new thing as it comes along.

As a drop of oil on the sea,
you must float,
using intellect and compassion
to ride the waves.

It seems to me, you have to think of significant
things to do together that require both of you. The

medieval idea of the gentle heart is very much a part of this. If what you've been calling love is really lust, that is a state alright: one that can die. Love doesn't die.

> For the gentle heart,
> marriage must first be spiritual,
> then comes physical consummation.

It's hard to talk about anything as sensitive as this, but that term "gentle heart" to me is a clue to what love is. The idea of the gentle heart involves a sense of responsibility to the person. If that is not there, you have not got love, you've got something else. If that *is* there, it will last. Lust doesn't, no responsibility there. In marriages that go when the children go, the parents' sense of responsibility was to the children, not to each other, and when that was gone, the link was gone.

Before there are any children or even before there is a marriage, the crucial question is: "Is this the gentle heart?" Is the person seeking a possession? Or is the person feeling a responsibility to the one with whom the relationship is taking place? If there is no feeling of responsibility, then I think you are in danger.

What I am saying is, not that responsibility constitutes love, but that love without a sense of responsibility is not love. It's taking possession. Are you trying to possess somebody? Or are you in a relationship?

Talking about what one has done in one's own life, I wouldn't have thought of marrying anyone unless, in committing myself to the marriage, I understood that I was taking that person's life in my hands. I can't understand that other feeling of possessing somebody. It is a failure to take responsibility for what the hell you are doing. One can have love affairs and all the weeping that goes on in all that, but that is very different from moving into a marriage.

In the first place, you have to know what you are doing. I think a lot of people don't know what they are doing, and they don't know what they're doing to that other person. If you don't have the maturity to control your compulsive passions, it seems to me that you are ineligible for marriage. I think what I am saying probably comes from my Catholic upbringing. In Catholicism, marriage is a destiny decision.

Beyond that, there was an omen in our marriage. I had a little twenty-dollar-a-year house in Woodstock, on a road called Maverick Road. We were driving up there for our honeymoon, and as we approached that road, a hearse came from the other side and drove before us. I had never seen a hearse in that neighborhood, and I read the omen as meaning we would be together until death. There it was.

What I see in marriage, then, is a real identification with that other person as your responsibility, and as the one whom you love. Committing yourself to anyone, turning your destiny over to a dual destiny, is a life commitment. To lose your sense of responsibility to the person who has given you that commitment because something comes along that enables you to think, "I'd like to fly off in this direction and forget that which has already been committed"—this is not marriage. I do not think you are married unless your relationship to your spouse has primary consideration in your life. It's got to be top.

Compulsive erotic relationships can break in on this. One is not in perfect control of oneself. I don't mean that everything outside of the marriage is lust. It can be love also. When you cut off a love that comes to you outside of marriage, you have cut off a part of yourself in the marriage.

But then you have the problem of relating with responsibility to that love affair and to the marriage that you've already got as your prime relationship, and that is not an easy thing to do. You have to develop a number of different ways of relating to people, not just one. Sometimes, if there is a mutual sense of the nature of the relationship and its value, then something can be worked out; but I would understand that, no matter what happened, the marriage would have to come back together again. It's prime. It's number one.

If the marriage is toxic, you have to decide whether there is a possibility of transforming the situation. If you feel that there can be a transformation, then you can go through the ordeal of effecting one. You can exert the necessary energy on the other to effect the transformation. That is to say, you can, as a kind of personal discipline, increase the atmosphere of love and confidence and cooperation. On the other hand, if your life is threatened, or even your love of life, and the situation cannot be transformed or you don't think it is worth the commitment, then you have got to clear out.

All of this depends, of course, on the individual case and one's own judgment. There are no basic rules that can be applied right across the board because the conflict situation differs in intensity and in character from case to case.

When I was a student in Germany, an old German professor said that the way to choose a wife is to look at her mother. If the mother is a good woman and the kind that you regard as ideal, then marry any one of her daughters, and she will shape a life for you.

> In marriage,
> the woman is the initiator,
> and the man rides along.

That idea of the wife being the one that shapes a life for you is one that I took to heart, and it's a good idea. The woman is the energy, the *sakti*, of life. The male must learn to ride on that energy and not dictate the life. I'm certain of that. He is the vehicle of the woman's energy. That's what he is. When the male won't disintegrate, you do not have a marriage. You have a living-together, perhaps, for practical or erotic reasons, but a marriage requires the dissolution of the male initiative.

> Marriage can't work without
> a psychological guiding of both people.

> There must be disintegration of ego
> for the two to combine.

> The uniting process involves
> fermentation, amalgamation,
> disintegration, and putrefaction
> in their psyches.

When I married Jean, I felt it was a crucifixion. The bridegroom does go to the bride as to the cross. The bride gives herself equally. It's a reciprocal crucifixion.

> In marriage
> you are not sacrificing yourself
> to the other person.
> You are sacrificing yourself
> to the relationship.

That's the problem with getting married. You must ask yourself, "Can I open myself to compassion?" Not to lust, but to compassion. I don't mean you have to have unconditional love. Committing yourself to a person unconditionally is very different from having unconditional love for everybody in New York City. I'm not the Dalai Lama, who's suppose to have unconditional love for everything in the world. Even God doesn't have unconditional love. He throws people into hell. I personally don't even think that unconditional love is an ideal. I think you've got to have a discriminating faculty and let bastards be bastards and let those that ought to be hit in the jaw get it. In fact, I have a list. If anybody has a working guillotine, I'd be glad to give them my list.

> When I look
> in the faces of my enemies,
> it makes me proud.

I think perhaps unconditional love is the Grail. The Grail is between God and the Devil, and it does not judge the way God judges. It goes past God—a pretty big picture. Love, which is unconditional in marriage, is specific; it is focused. It is for *that* person and not for somebody else. Unconditional love goes right through everything, and it's a breakthrough in spiritual life. Do not look for it outside of yourself. The only place to look for it is inside. If it is going to be unconditional love, what's out there doesn't matter.

The key to the Grail is compassion,
suffering with, feeling another's sorrow
as if it were your own.

The one who finds
the dynamo of compassion
is the one who's found the Grail.

The question is: "Can I open myself to compassion?" Compassion for me is just what the word says: it is "suffering with." It is an immediate participation in the suffering of another to such a degree that you forget yourself and your own safety and spontaneously do what's necessary.

I think this has something to do with what's meant by the image of the Grail, since the thing that effected the healing of the Grail King was the spontaneous act of asking that question and not withholding it. Often you feel that such a spontaneous act will make a fool out of you and so you don't do it—I will look like a fool if I do that. That's the failure in the Grail Castle.

"How is it possible that suffering that is neither my own nor of my concern should immediately affect me as though it were my own, and with such force that it moves me to action?" —Schopenhauer[16]

And in the third chapter of *Ulysses,* Joyce writes that Stephen, as he walked along the seashore, asked himself essentially this question: Would I forget my own self-protection to the extent of risking a swim out there and be at the mercy of someone whose power out there I wouldn't know anything about? When you rescue someone from drowning, you never know if they'll pull you down with them.

"This is something really mysterious, something for which Reason can provide no explanation, and for which no basis can be found in practical experience. It is nevertheless of common occurrence, and everyone has had the experience. It is not unknown even to the most hard-hearted and self-interested. Examples appear every day before our eyes of instant responses of this kind, without reflection, one person helping another, coming to his aid, even setting his own life in clear danger for someone whom he has seen for the first time, having nothing more in mind than that the other is in need and in peril of his life." —Schopenhauer[17]

There was an article in the New York papers a few months ago about a kid who dove into the Hudson River to save a drowining dog and then had to be saved himself. When asked why he'd dove in, he said, "Because it was my dog." Then there was the girl who went into a burning building—twice—to save her little brother and sister, and when she was asked why she'd done that, she said, "Because I loved them."

Such a one is then acting, Schopenhauer answers, out of an instinctive recognition of the truth that he and that other in fact are one. He has been moved not from the lesser, secondary knowledge of himself as separate from the others, but from an immediate experience of the greater, truer truth, that we are all one in the ground of our being.[18]

That's the power. These people didn't know if they had the strength or not. It's not duty, not reckoning. It is a flash: a breakthrough of the reality of this life that lives in us. At such moments, you realize that you and that other are, in fact, one. It's a big realization.

> Survival is the second law of life.
> The first is that we are all one.

*I*T *is possible to observe, in the earliest phases of the development of the infant, symptoms of a dawning "mythology" of a state beyond the vicissitudes of time. These appear as reactions to, and spontaneous defenses against, the body-destructive fantasies that assail the child when it is deprived of the mother's breast.[19] "The infant reacts with a temper tantrum and the fantasy that goes with the temper tantrum is to tear everything out of the mother's body. ...The child then fears retaliation for these impulses, i.e., that everything will be scooped out of its own inside."[20] Anxieties for the integrity of its body, fantasies of restitution, a silent, deep requirement for indestructibility and protection against the "bad" forces from within and without, begin to direct the shaping psyche; and these remain as determining factors in the later neurotic, and even normal, life activities, spiritual efforts, religious beliefs, and ritual practices of the adult.[21]*

The myths are clues
to unite the forces within us.

And so we have...this critical problem as human beings of seeing to it that the mythology—the constellation of sign signals, affect images, energy-releasing and -directing signs— that we are communicating to our young will deliver directive messages qualified to relate them richly and vitally to the environment that is to be theirs for life, and not to some period of man already past, some piously desiderated future, or—what is worst of all—some querulous, freakish sect or momentary fad. And I call this problem critical because, when it is badly resolved, the result for the miseducated individual is what is known, in mythological terms, as a Waste Land situation. The world does not talk to him; he does not talk to the world. When that is the case, there is a cut-off, the individual is thrown back on himself, and he is in prime shape for that psychotic break-away that will turn him into either an essential schizophrenic in a padded cell, or a paranoid screaming slogans at large, in a bughouse without walls.[22]

Myth makes a connection between our waking consciousness and the mystery of the universe. It gives us a map or picture of the universe and allows us to see ourselves in relationship to nature, as when we speak of Father Sky and Mother Earth. It supports and validates a certain social and moral order. The Ten Commandments being given to Moses by God on Mount Sinai is an example of this. Lastly, it helps us pass through and deal with the various stages of life from birth to death.

We have, consequently, the comparatively complex problem in educating our young of training them not simply to assume uncritically the patterns of the past, but to recognize and cultivate their own creative possibilities; not to remain on some proven level of earlier biology and sociology, but to represent a movement of the species forward.[23]

Basically, everyone needs a father. The father has a vital role. The mother represents nature, but the father introduces the son and daughter to social relationships.

> From your mother you get your body.
> From your father you get
> your role in the social world.

The son has to play a role like that of his father, so the father is a model, either a positive or a negative one. You may be disgusted with the kind of life your father lives, but you have that model, and responding negatively to it will be your life. If he's not there, it's almost impossible to relate effectively from where you are in your family to the outside world.

For the girl, the father is the first intimate relationship to the male principle in some way or other. With the father gone, the mother must play both roles, and I think the child, down deep, blames the mother for there being no father there. It's a sense of "you have deprived me of the person who would have been absolutely my guide and my messenger."

MONEY is congealed energy and releasing it releases life possibilities. You realize that the possibilities of life in an economically oriented society are really a function of how much money you've got.

On the other hand, money has never meant anything to me. I got back from my student years in Europe three weeks before the Wall Street crash. The only money I had was what I'd made playing in a jazz band in college. I'd earned several thousand dollars—which was a lot in those days—and that was what I had until it disappeared. I didn't make another cent for five years. I found that, if you had no responsibilities, you could live wonderfully without any money. In fact, I thought anybody who worked for money was a fool. I took a vow never to do anything for money. Now, that does not mean that when I do something for somebody I don't ask for money. I want as much as I can get, but that's the secondary part of the game. My life course is absolutely indifferent to money. As a result, a lot of money has come in by my doing what I feel I want to do from the inside. If you do that, you are doing things that attract money, because you are giving life and life responds in the way of its counterpart in hard coin.

> If you follow your bliss,
> you will always have your bliss,
> money or not.

If you follow money,
you may lose it,
and you will have nothing.

Being as I was, and given the field I was interested in, I had a certain disdain for people who gave their lives to making money. Now that I have made money, in dealing with it I've had to be in touch with people whose business is money, whose whole life has been in that field, and I've had an interesting and surprising experience: I've met some magnificent people.

Money experienced as life energy is indeed a meditation, and letting it flow out instead of hoarding it is a mode of participation in the lives of others. There's a beautiful thing that can grow out of a life devoted to money that surprised me.

In the living of a life today, money is a facilitating energy source. With money in the tank like gasoline, you can get places you other wise couldn't go.

You've got to use the advantages that you have cultivated. Otherwise, if you drop those, you are going to have a negative reaction in ten years or so. What I mean is, as you go from threshold to threshold, it must be the same you that makes the jump. You don't go down again, you start from where you are. From that, more and more will blossom. The potentialities from your center are used for further extrapolation in the next venture.

From what I have seen in the history of the arts in New York, when money is poured on something it flowers. With money there has to be a flow. I had a beautiful experience of a man with money when I was a trustee of the Bollingen Foundation, which was founded by Paul Mellon, an enormously wealthy man. He and his wife had been in analysis with Carl Jung when the war came and they had to leave Switzerland. They asked Jung what they could give him in the way of a gift to express their gratitude for what he had done. He suggested they establish a foundation for the interpretation and study of symbols. That's what they did, and it is an example of a lot of money being put to the right use. The influence of that Bollingen Series on the literature and science of America has been enormous. Without that money it would never have happened.

You have to have not only the energy, but also the capacity of mind that gives the model of the channel—with that, life really flowers. When you put the money in the wrong place. It can be devastating. Where is the money going and where is it coming from in the economy of a nation, the economy of a city? That's one of the big problems. You can turn a flowering culture into a desiccating culture just by wrong channeling.

I always think you can translate sociology into psychology. It has to do with energy distribution. What are you going to do with your money? What factor in your own consciousness are you going to favor in the spending of the money? For instance, I have a seventy-five-dollar book coming out. Some people will say that is expensive, but those same people will spend one-hundred-and-fifty dollars to have dinner in a restaurant with another couple. So, is the money going up here in your mind or is it going down here in your stomach? Up here, you can't replace the book I would have given you; but down here, you could have bought cheaper food that would have been just as nourishing.

IF you're getting a degree to compensate for an inferiority complex, give up the complex, because it's an artificial thing.

When you're going for a degree, you don't do what *you* want to do. You find out what the professor wants you to do to get the degree, and you just do it. If you want a degree so you can teach, the idea is to get the degree in the quickest, easiest way. When you have it, *then* you can expand and get your education.

I was given a fellowship to go to Europe, and I went to the University of Paris. I was working on medieval French and Provençal and on the troubadour poetry. When I got to Europe, I discovered Modern Art: James Joyce, Picasso, Mondrian—the whole bunch of them. Paris in 1927–28 was something else. Then I went to Germany and started studying Sanskrit and got all involved in Hinduism. I discovered Jung while in Germany. Everything was opening up—this way, that way. Well, my question then was, "Am I going to go back into that bottle?" My interest in Celtic Romance was gone.

I went to the university and said, "Listen, I don't want to get back into that bottle." I had put in all the hours necessary for the degree; all I had to do was write that goddamn thesis. They wouldn't let me move into another place and continue my education, so I said to hell with it. I went up into the woods and spent five years reading. I never got the Ph.D. I learned to live on absolutely nothing. I was free and had no responsibilities. It was marvelous.

> It takes courage
> to do what you want.
>
> Other people
> have a lot of plans for you.
>
> Nobody wants you to do
> what you want to do.
>
> They want you to go on their trip,
> but you can do what you want.
>
> I did. I went into the woods
> and read for five years.

It was from 1929 to 1934, five years. I went up to a little shack in Woodstock, New York, and just dug in. All I did was read, read, read, and take notes. It was during the Great Depression. I didn't have any money, but there was an important book firm in New York called Stechert-Hafner, and I would write to them for books—the books of Frobenius were expensive—and they'd send me copies, and I wouldn't pay. That was the way people behaved during the depression. They waited until I got a job, and then I paid them. That was noble. I really appreciated that.

I read Joyce and Mann and Spengler. Spengler speaks about Nietzsche. I go to Nietzsche. I then find you can't read Nietzsche until you've read Schopenhauer, so I go to Schopenhauer. I find you can't read Schopenhauer until you've read Kant. Then I go to Kant—well, okay, you can start there, but it's tough going. Then Goethe.

The exciting thing was to see that Joyce was actually dealing with the same material. He never mentions the name of Schopenhauer, but I can prove he was a major figure in Joyce's construction of his system. Then I read Jung, and I see that the structure of his thinking is basically the same as that of Spengler's, and I'm putting all this stuff together...

I don't know what it was during those five years, but I was convinced I would still be alive for a little while. I remember one time when I had a dollar bill in the top drawer of a little chest, and I knew as long as that was there I still had resources. It was great. I had no responsibilities, none. It was exciting—writing journals, trying to find out what I wanted. I still have those things. When I look into them now, I can't believe it.

Actually, there were times when I almost thought —*almost* thought—"Jeez, I wish someone would tell me what I *had* to do," that kind of thing. Freedom involves making decisions, and each decision is a destiny decision. It's very difficult to find in the outside world something that matches what the system inside you is yearning for. My feeling now is that I had a perfect life: what I needed came along just when I needed it. What I needed then was life without a job for five years. It was fundamental.

As Schopenhauer says, when you look back on your life, it looks as though it were a plot, but when you are into it, it's a mess: just one surprise after another. Then, later, you see it was perfect. So, I have a theory that if you are on your own path things are going to come to you. Since it's your own path, and no one has ever been on it before, there's no precedent, so everything that happens is a surprise and is timely.

In the midst of my time in Woodstock, I decided I would look for a job. I had a little Model A Ford, and I drove it across the continent right in the middle of the Great Depression. I will never forget that drive. I'd pass automobiles on the road that had broken down with whole families in them. It was awful. People of today have no notion of what went on at that time.

When I started driving to the west coast from New York in that car, I drove down through Virginia and stopped at a beautiful natural bridge. I spent two hours just walking back and forth in that natural bridge area, thinking how George Washington was a surveyor here and all that kind of thing. Somehow I felt that it was teaching me something, that I was learning something. I put it in my diary as a very important experience.

When I arrived out here, there was no job, and when you get to California, you can't keep driving west. On a boat back from Hawaii in 1925, I had met a girl who was living in San Jose. We'd kept a long-range correspondence, little postcards from here and there. I was going down to Carmel, so I thought, "Why not drop in on Idell and just say 'Hi.'" So I dropped in— "Hello, hello, hello." "You're going down to Carmel? Let me go down with you. My sister Carol's down there. She's married a chap who wants to be a writer. I'll introduce you."

Her sister was married to John Steinbeck, so I met him. And I discovered a world of wonderful people sitting around wondering what to do next. The people in this crowd were John and Carol Steinbeck, Rich Lovejoy and his wife, Natalya—"Tal," who was doing Steinbeck's typing—and Ed Rickets—"Doc" in John's novels. Rich and Tal are the couple in *Cannery Row*.

By the way, that party in *Cannery Row* was given for me—Steinbeck put another cast of characters in it.

Nobody, except Ed, had a job or anything of the kind. Everybody was "without any strings," you know, just flopping around. Steinbeck was writing and writing and writing. He'd just finished a book called *Pastures of Heaven* and was starting *To A God Unknown*. When I arrived, the first thing he said was, "Come, let me read you the first chapter of my book." I was twenty-eight, and he was about thirty-four or -five. He found me a place to live, a tiny little house on 4th Street called the Canary Cottage, right next to a house owned by Ed.

When you're at a loss, you're really at a loss. I had no philosophy. I had no anything after Columbia—we had been studying John Dewey for God's sake. In the Carmel library, my hand went up to a book in two volumes, *Decline of the West* by Oswald Spengler, and, boy, that was the thunderbolt. Spengler says, "Young man, if you want to be in the world of the future, put your paintbrush and poet's pen on the shelf and pick up the monkey wrench or the law book." I said to Steinbeck, "Listen, you have to read this thing." When I had finished the first volume, I gave it to him. He came back a little while later and said, "Oh, I can't read this. Oh—my art." He was knocked out for about two weeks and couldn't write.

One day, after he had recovered from the paragraph in Spengler, he was walking around, rubbing his sides, saying, "I feel creative." Steinbeck was always going around rubbing his sides. He loved to rub his sides. Another day, he came in and said, "I've sold *Pastures of Heaven,* and they want my next two books." Well, I know now that every publisher who takes your first book wants your next two, because they're not going to advertise you and then lose you to somebody else. That was a great day, so we had a party.

After I'd read Spengler's book, which was a major experience for me, I said to Ed, "Say, Ed, you know, I've been saying 'no' to life all my life, and I think I'd better begin saying 'yes.'" He said, "Well, the way to do that is to get drunk. Let's have a party." It was in the middle of, not only the Depression, but also Prohibition. He said, "I'll use my laboratory alcohol, and we'll put something together."

Jesus, that was a night! He mixed this concoction of fruit juice and alcohol in a bowl. Then he put that bowl in a larger bowl, and put salted ice around it to keep it cold. We started the party around four in the afternoon, and at three o'clock in the morning, a police car pulled up to the front door and two cops came in. They said, "What's going on here?" Well, Steinbeck knew them, so he said, "We're having a party. Here, have a drink." Now we had stopped drinking about an hour before, and meanwhile, the center bowl had shipped salt water, so it was now alcohol, fruit juice, and salt water. Well, when those two cops tasted that drink, they just looked at us as if to say, "What the hell are you people drinking here?" And that was that.

Ed Rickets was the only one who had work. He had a laboratory and collected sea cucumbers and little jellyfish and so forth for schools. He'd fertilize a group of starfish eggs, and then cut them off at different stages to show the whole series for a biology class. When the tide was low where there was good catching —for instance, up at Santa Cruz—we would all go off to collect these damned things for Ed.

He was great with animals. He had two rattle-snakes in a box in the lab, and he invited us all down one day to see him feed white mice to the snakes. Well, this was something. Steinbeck actually wrote a short story about it. Here's this snake that's been asleep for weeks—snakes with nothing to do are like that. Ed drops this white mouse in the cage with the snake, and we're all gathered around to watch. Somehow, you're automatically on the mouse's side. The little mouse sniffs around and goes up the length of the snake, and finally he gets the idea that this isn't a good place to be, so he goes into the corner and sits there. The rattlesnake looks at the mouse, moves over, and —"Bing!"—hits it. Two little red spots appear on the mouse's nose, and it just spins up and flops back. So, the mouse is dead, and the snake is alive, so now you're on the side of the rattlesnake trying to eat that mouse—the mouse is bigger around than the snake's diameter.

Ed says, "Now watch him. He's going to unhook his jaws." He unhooks his jaws and begins injesting the mouse—you could see it changing shape in the snake's mouth, because the saliva has digestive qualities. I tell you, you felt it right in your throat. The most absurd moment was when the rattlesnake got tired, and there was nothing left but two legs and a tail sticking out of its mouth. But presently that went down too.

Every detail of those years stands out in my memory. In Goethe's wonderful book *Wilhelm Meister's Student Years*, and again in *Wilhelm Meister's Wander Years*, there's the idea of bumping into experience and people while you're wandering. You really are experiencing life that way. Nothing is routine, nothing is taken for granted. Everything is standing out on it's own, because everything is a possibility, everything is a clue, everything is talking to you. It's marvelous. It's as though you had a nose that brought you into the right places. You are in for wonderful moments when you travel like that—for example, my putting up my hand in the Carmel library and finding a book that became a destiny book. It really did! That rambling is a chance to sniff things out and somehow get a sense of where you feel you can settle.

The poor chap who gets himself in a job and goes down that groove all his life....A friend gave me a list of things that let you know you are old. Some of them are silly, others are serious. One is "...when you sink your teeth into a juicy steak and they stay there." Another is "...when your back goes out more often than you do." "...When you see a pretty girl, the garage door flies open responding to your pacemaker." The really serious one is "...when you've gotten to the top of the ladder and find it's against the wrong wall." And that's where so many people are. It's dreadful. And then, Jesus, to descend the whole ladder and start up another... Forget the ladder and just wander, bump around.

I spent eight months rambling. I studied Russian for no reason except that it was the next language to learn after I'd learned Spanish, French, and German. I read *War and Peace* in Russian. I can't read two words in Russian now, but it got me into the Russian community in Los Angeles, where there were lots of people who'd come here after the revolution. It was wonderful. Then I got into my car and went somewhere else.

After a year in California, I returned to New York to take a job in a prep school. I was paid nine-hundred dollars for teaching the boys corrective German and French, Ancient History, and English. Meanwhile, I was their nursemaid: I put them to bed at night, got them up in the morning, made them obey, and then took them out on the athletic field. I'll tell you, that was another kind of life, and I couldn't take it. I was in a beautiful school, a beautiful job, but I knew I was off the rails. I went right back on the Depression.

Oh, those were grand experiences. I was just flopping around, sniffing out what I would do and what I wouldn't do. I only wanted to do what made sense to my interior. I don't see how one can live otherwise. And nothing is better than reading when there is nothing else to do.

When you wander, think of what you want to do *that* day, not what you told yourself you were going to want to do. And there are two things you must not worry about when you have no responsibilities: one is being hungry, and the other is what people will think of you. Wandering time is positive. Don't think of new things, don't think of achievement, don't think of anything of the kind. Just think, "Where do I feel good? What is giving me joy?"

I mean it. This is simply basic. Get those pressure ideas out of your system, and then you can find, like a ball on a roulette wheel, where you are going to land. The roulette ball doesn't say, "Well, people will think better of me over there than over there." Take what comes and be where you like. What counts is being where you feel you're in *your* place. What people think is *their* problem.

"What will they think of me?"
—must be put aside for bliss.

My parents never pushed me around. I had special luck there. By the time I was invited to teach at Sarah Lawrence, I had decided that I didn't need a job and did not want one. It would interrupt my reading. But when I saw that school full of gorgeous girls, I thought, "Well this is alright." When I finally got that job, I was thirty years old, and Dad said, "Joe, I thought you were going to be a literary bum." But until I got the job, he never said a word. He was a good father. When *The Hero with a Thousand Faces* came out, he said, "I prophesy this is going to be a wonderful book." He hadn't read a word of it, but he knew his boy had done it.

I know that wandering might seem a strange form of life to someone with a science background, which tends to give you a prospect out ahead of what you're doing, but while wandering, you experience a kind of mysteriously organic process. It's like a tree growing. It doesn't know where it's growing next. A branch may grow out this way, then that way, and then another way. If you let it be that way and don't have pressures from outside, when you look back, you'll see that this will have been an organic development. Just remember: Parzival blew the job when he did what people expected him to do.

THE Grail Hero—*particularly in the person of Perceval or Parzival, the "Great Fool"—is the forthright, simple, uncorrupted, noble son of nature, without guile, strong in the purity of the yearning of his heart. In the words of the poet Wolfram von Eschenbach...describing his Grail Hero's childhood in the forest: "Of sorrow he knew nothing, unless it was the birdsong above him; for the sweetness of it pierced his heart and made his little bosom swell: His nature and his yearning so compelled him."[24] His widowed, noble mother, in their forest retreat had told him of God and Satan, "distinguished for him dark and light."[25] However, in his own deeds light and dark were mixed. He was not an angel or a saint, but a living, questing man of deeds, gifted with paired virtues of courage and compassion, to which was added loyalty. And it was through his steadfastness in these—not supernatural grace—that he won, at last, to the Grail.[26]*

Parzival makes two visits to the Grail Castle. The first is a failure. The Grail King is a wounded man, whose nature has been broken by castration in a battle. Parzival spontaneously wishes to ask him, "What is wrong?" But then, he has been told that a knight does not ask questions, and so, in order to preserve the image of himself as a noble knight, he restrains his natural impulse of compassion, and the Grail quest fails.

...in the end, as in the case of Parzival, the guide within will be his own noble heart alone, and the guide without, the image of beauty, the radiance of divinity, that wakes in his heart amor: *the deepest, inmost seed of his nature, consubstantial with the process of the All, "thus come." And in this life-creative adventure the criterion of achievement will be...the courage to let go the past, with its truths, its goals, its dogmas of "meaning," and its gifts: to die to the world and come to birth from within.*[27]

> The twelfth century
> is the follow-your-bliss time.

What the Holy Grail symbolizes is the highest spiritual fulfillment of a human life. Each life has some kind of high fulfillment, and each has its own gift from the Grail. The theme of compassion is part of the clue about how to get there and where it is. It has to do with overcoming the same temptations that the Buddha overcame: of attachment to this, that, or the other life detail that has pulled you off course.

What pulls you off from spiritual fulfillment? I know when my life is not in the center. I get desirously involved with my relation to some achievement or system that is tangential to the real centering of my life. And I know when I'm on track—that is, when everything is in a harmonious relationship to what I regard as the best I've got in me.

In the Grail legends, the land of people doing what they think they ought to do or have to do is the wasteland. What is the wasteland to you? I know damned well what the wasteland would be to me: the academic approach to my material; or a marriage to someone who had no thoughts or feelings for me or my work. Living with such a person would be the wasteland.

I find working for money to be the wasteland—
doing something that somebody else wants instead of
the thing that is my next step. I have been guided all
along by a strong revulsion from any sort of action that
does not correspond to the impulse of my own wish.

> The person of noble heart
> acts spontaneously
> and will avoid the wasteland,
> the world of "Thou Shalt."

*"I will not serve that in which I no longer believe
whether it call itself my home, my fatherland, or my
church....And I am not afraid to make a mistake, even a
great mistake, a lifelong mistake, and perhaps as long as
eternity too."* —Stephen Dedalus[28]

The crucial thing to live for is the sense of life in
what you are doing, and if that is not there, then you
are living according to other peoples' notions of how
life should be lived.

The opposite to doing what you think you ought to
do is compassion. The one who finds the Grail is symbolic of the one who has come to that place and whose
life is of compassion. The one who finds as his motiva-
tion the dynamism of his compassion has found the
Grail. That means spontaneous recognition of the identity of I and Thou. This is the Grail center.

*To become—in Jung's terms—individuated, to live as a
released individual, one has to know how and when to put
on and to put off the masks of one's various life roles....The
aim of individuation requires that one should find and then
learn to live out of one's own center, in control of one's for
and against. And this cannot be achieved by enacting and
responding to any general masquerade of fixed roles.*[29]

Parzival achieves the Grail Castle, and Galahad beholds the Grail. These are two totally different Grail traditions. Parzival is the fulfilled, secular man. Galahad is the monastic, chaste knight, who has insulated himself from life.

In the story of Sir Galahad, the knights agree to go on a quest, but thinking it would be a disgrace to go forth in a group, each "entered into the forest, at one point or another, there where they saw it to be thickest, all in those places where they found no way or path."[30] Where there is a way or a path, it's someone else's way. Each knight enters the forest at the most mysterious point and follows his own intuition. What each brings forth is what never before was on land or sea: the fulfillment of his unique potentialities, which are different from anybody else's. All you get on your life way are little clues.

In that wonderful story, when any knight sees the trail of another, thinks he's getting there, and starts to follow the other's track, he goes astray entirely.

"In the last analysis, every life is the realization of a whole, that is, of a self, for which reason this realization can be called 'individuation.' All life is bound to individual carriers who realize it, and it is simply inconceivable without them. But every carrier is charged with an individual destiny and destination, and the realization of this alone makes sense of life."—Jung[31]

In all traditional systems, whether of the Orient or of the Occident, the authorized mythological forms are presented in rites to which the individual is expected to respond with an experience of commitment and belief. But suppose he fails to do so? Suppose the entire inheritance of mythological, theological, and philosophical forms fails to wake in him any authentic response of this kind? How then is he to behave? The normal way is to fake it, to feel oneself to be inadequate, to pretend to believe, to strive to believe, and to live, in the imitation of others, an inauthentic life. The authentic creative way, on the other hand, which I would term the way of art as opposed to religion, is, rather, to reverse this authoritative order.[32]

As in the novels of Joyce, so in those of Mann, the key to the progression lies in the stress on what is inward....In the words of Joyce's hero: "When the soul of a man is born in this country there are nets flung at it to hold it back from flight. You talk to me of nationality, language, religion. I shall try to fly by those nets."[33]

For what to the soul are nets, "flung at it to hold it back from flight," can become for the one who has found his own center the garment, freely chosen, of his further adventure.[34]

What kind of action and life experience would be appropriate for one who has had this fulfilling moment of the Grail experience? There are no rules for what you do. Buddha came back and taught for fifty years. To answer such a question, one would have to predict the circumstances of the life that one would enter.

Once you've achieved the experience, you have to achieve it the next second and the next second also. The process of achievement comes in translating the experiences of life into that eternal elixir, which is the "happy with Him forever in Heaven" part of the answer to the penny catechism question: "Why did God make you?" The answer I learned was: "God made me to know Him, to love Him, and to serve Him in this world, and to be happy with Him forever in Heaven." Translating that into metaphor: Heaven is the symbol of the eternal life that is within you. It's a basic aspect of yourself forever. That's the rapture. And then, temporal life asks for "knowing, loving, and serving... God," the generating energy of the life that is within you and all things.

My experience is that I can feel that I'm in the Grail Castle when I'm living with people I love, doing what I love. I get that sense of being fulfilled. But, by god, it doesn't take much to make me feel I've lost the Castle, it's gone. One way to lose the Grail is to go to a cocktail party. That's my idea of not being there at all.

My sense of it is that you have to keep working to get there. It may take a little while. Even when you have gotten there, it's easy to get flipped out, because the world has things it wants you to do and you have decided not to do what the world wants. The problem is to find a field of action to give you that inner satisfaction so that you're not thrown out.

...not all, even today, are of that supine sort that must have their life values given them, cried at them from the pulpits and other mass media of the day. For there is, in fact, in quiet places, a great deal of deep spiritual quest and finding now in progress in this world, outside the sanctified social centers, beyond their purview and control: in small groups, here and there, and more often, more typically (as anyone who looks around may learn), by ones and twos, there entering the forest at those points which they themselves have chosen, where they see it to be most dark, and there is no beaten way or path.[35]

The hero's journey always begins with the call. One way or another, a guide must come to say, "Look, you're in Sleepy Land. Wake. Come on a trip. There is a whole aspect of your consciousness, your being, that's not been touched. So you're at home here? Well, there's not enough of you there." And so it starts.

The herald or announcer of the adventure...is often dark, loathly, or terrifying, judged evil by the world; yet if one could follow, the way would be opened through the walls of day into the dark where the jewels glow.[36]

The call is to leave a certain social situation, move into your own loneliness and find the jewel, the center that's impossible to find when you're socially engaged. You are thrown off-center, and when you feel off-center, it's time to go. This is the departure when the hero feels something has been lost and goes to find it. You are to cross the threshold into new life. It's a dangerous adventure, because you are moving out of the sphere of the knowledge of you and your community.

The first step, detachment or withdrawal, consists in a radical transfer of emphasis from the external to the internal world, macro- to microcosm, a retreat from the desperations of the waste land to the peace of the everlasting realm that is within. But this realm, as we know from psychoanalysis, is precisely the infantile unconscious. It is the realm that we enter in sleep. We carry it within ourselves forever. All the ogres and secret helpers of our nursery are there, all the magic of childhood. And more important, all the life-potentialities that we never managed to bring to adult realization, those other portions of ourself, are there; for such golden seeds do not die.[37]

When one thinks of some reason for not going or has fear and remains in society because it's safe, the results are radically different from what happens when one follows the call. If you refuse to go, then you are someone else's servant. When this refusal of the call happens, there is a kind of drying up, a sense of life lost. Everything in you knows that a required adventure has been refused. Anxieties build up. What you have refused to experience in a positive way, you will experience in a negative way.

If what you are following, however, is your own true adventure, if it is something appropriate to your deep spiritual need or readiness, then magical guides will appear to help you. If you say, "Everyone's going on this trip this year, and I'm going too," then no guides will appear. Your adventure has to be coming right out of your own interior. If you are ready for it, then doors will open where there were no doors before, and where there would not be doors for anyone else. And you must have courage. It's the call to adventure, which means there is no security, no rules.

When you cross the threshold, you are passing into the dark forest, taking a plunge into the sea, embarking upon the night sea journey. It involves passing through clashing rocks, narrow gates, or the like, which represent yes and no, the pairs of opposites. There will be a moment when the walls of the world seem to open for a second, and you get an insight through. Jump then! Go! The gates will often close so fast that they take off the tail of your horse. You may be dismembered, lose everything you have. This is Christ leaving the Mother, the world, and going to the Father, the Spirit. This is Jonah swallowed by the whale, its jaws being the pairs of opposites.

What this represents psychologically is the trip from the realm of conscious, rational intentions into the zone of those energies of the body that are moving from another center: the center with which you are trying to get in touch.

As you now go towards the center, there will come more aids, as well as increasingly difficult trials. You have to give up more and more of what you're hanging on to. The final thing is a total giving up, a yielding all the way. This is a place directly opposite to your life experiences and all that you've been taught in school. Psychologically, it's a shift into the unconscious; otherwise, it's a move into a field of action of which you know nothing. Anything can happen, and it may be favorable or unfavorable.

The deeper you go, and the closer you get to the final realization, the heavier the resistance. You are coming down to those areas that are the ones that are repressed, and it's that repression system that you have to pass through. And there, of course, is where magical aid is most required. The hero may here discover for the first time that there is everywhere a benign power supporting him in his superhuman passage.

You come then to the final experience of discovering and making your own that which was lacking in the place from which you departed. This experience can be rendered in four different ways.

One rendition is the *Sacred Marriage*, the meeting with the beloved which brings the birth of your own spiritual life, with the bride being whatever the life is that your relating to: male/female, I/Thou, this/that.

Another rendering is *Atonement with the Father*. The son has been separated from the father, meaning he has been living a life that's inappropriate to his real heritage. The son is the temporal aspect, and the father is the eternal aspect of the same being. The father represents the natural order from which you have been removed. You are trying to find your character, which you inherit from your father. Atonement is bringing your own personal and contemporary program into accord with the life momentum out of which you have come.

Then there is *Apotheosis*, the realization that "I am that which all these other beings are." The hero knows that he is It, the Buddha image, the knower of the truth. "The Kingdom of the Father is spread upon the earth and men do not see it." That's the illumination that comes with Apotheosis. You are not allowed that realization in Christianity, except in Gnostic Christianity. You can't say, "The Christhood is in me."

Finally there's the *Elixir Theft*, an entirely different sort of realization. Instead of a slow progress through the mysteries with the good will of the powers, there is a violent pressure through and a seizing—the fire theft by Prometheus or the use of LSD in the 60s—and you flee from the powers that you did not appease on the way. This is the transformation flight, where the hero, with the powers after him, carries his goods back to the light world as fast as he can. Or one can have a schizophrenic crack up and stay down there.

The two worlds, the divine and the human, can be pictured only as distinct from each other—different as life and death, as day and night. The hero adventures out of the land we know into darkness; there he accomplishes his adventure, or again is simply lost to us, imprisoned, or in danger; and his return is described as a coming back out of that yonder zone. Nevertheless—and here is a great key to the understanding of myth and symbol—the two kingdoms are actually one. The realm of the gods is a forgotten dimension of the world we know.[38]

An image of the return that amuses me is that of a young man who comes from Wisconsin to New York to study art. He's gone into Greenwich Village, the underworld of Manhattan. He has a number of nymphs to help him and a master with whom he is studying. He finally achieves an art style. Then, having achieved his style, he comes to 57th Street with his paintings, and he meets the cold eye of the dealer.

> The great problem is bringing life
> back into the wasteland,
> where people live inauthentically.

Bringing back the gift to integrate it into a rational life is very difficult. It is even more difficult than going down into the underworld. What you have to bring back is something that the world lacks—which is why you went to get it—and lacking it, the world does not know that it needs it. And so, on the return, when you come with your boon for the world and there is no reception, what are you going to do? There are three possible reactions.

One answer is to say, "To hell with them, I'm going back to the woods." You buy yourself a dog and a pipe and let the weeds grow in the gate. You have come back to the world with your gift, and people look at you with glassy eyes, call you "a kook," and so you retreat. This is refusal of the return.

The second way is to say, "What do they want?" You have a skill. You can give them what they want, the commercial way. Then you have created a whole pitch for your expressivity, and what you had before gets lost. You have a public career, and you have renounced the jewel.

The third possibility is to try to find some aspect of the domain into which you have come that can receive a little portion of what you have to give. You try to find a means to deliver what you have found as the life boon in terms and in proportions that are proper to the world's ability to receive. It requires a good deal of compassion and patience. Look for cracks in the wall and give only to those who are ready for your jewel.

If all else fails, you can get a job teaching and introduce your message to the people who are studying with you. If you can get one little hook into the given society, you will find presently that you are able to deliver your message. Artists who teach are an example of this: they are doing their creative work, but they are being sustained by something that is secondary to their primary job. They are receiving adequate income and gradually build up a following.

You do not have a complete adventure unless you do get back. There is a time to go into the woods and a time to come back, and you know which it is. Do you have the courage? It takes a hell of a lot of courage to return after you've been in the woods.

Those are modes of having this realization, and the final thing is knowing, loving, and serving life in a way in which you are eternally at rest. That point of rest has got to be in all of it. Even though you are active out there in the world, within you there's a point of complete composure and rest. When that's not there, then you are in agony.

> When the world
> seems to be falling apart,
> the rule is to hang onto your own bliss.
> It's that life that survives.

Freedom to pass back and forth across the world division ...is the talent of the master. The Cosmic Dancer, declares Nietzsche, does not rest heavily in a single spot, but gaily, lightly, turns and leaps from one position to another.[39]

*T*HERE *is a Japanese saying I recall once having heard, of the five stages of a man's growth: "At ten, an animal; at twenty, a lunatic; at thirty, a failure; at forty, a fraud; at fifty, a criminal." And at sixty, I would add (since by that time one will have gone through all this), one begins advising one's friends; and at seventy (realizing that everything said has been misunderstood) one keeps quiet and is taken for a sage. "At eighty," then said Confucius, "I knew my ground and stood firm."* [40]

Jung speaks of the curve of a lifetime being divided in half: the first half is the time of relationships, and the second half is the time of finding the sense of life within; or, as the Hindus say, "following the *marga*"—the path, the footsteps of the human experience you've had—to your own inward life. And then, total disengagement. Going through the last passage without anxiety, without fear.

You go to your death singing.

"As a physician I am convinced that it is hygienic...to discover in death a goal toward which one can strive; and that shrinking away from it is something unhealthy and abnormal which robs the second half of life of its purpose."—Jung [41]

It is important to know how old you are in spiritual development, where you are on this path. The function of initiations is to commit one's whole psychological pitch to the requirements of a particular stage in life. The big initiation is when one has to leave the psychology of childhood behind: the death of the infantile ego, which is dependant and obedient, and the birth of the self-reliant adult participating in the society.

The first quarter of life is that of student, and the ideal there is obedience—"comeliness of appearance and sweetness of conduct," according to Dante—and this would mean conforming generally to the patterns required by the society. This interval is what Nietzsche calls the period of the camel, for the camel gets down on his knees and asks to have a load put on him.

The second quarter is that of householder; that is to say, you have moved into the responsibilities of adult life. In the Indian system, your responsibilities are dictated in terms of the *dharma,* the law of your social order. In our society, you voluntarily choose your responsibilities, and it is through the assumption of those responsibilities, whatever they may be, that you achieve your position, name, and fame in the world. Making such choices involves a development of the ego function, the function of independent evaluation, and your assumption of tasks and positions is relevant to your own value determinations. This period is the age of the dragon on whose every scale are emblazoned the words "Thou Shalt."

Midlife is typically the period, not of achievement, but of realization, and it should be the period of fulfillment. In Nietzsche's stages, when the camel is well-loaded, it gets to its feet and goes out into the desert and turns into a lion. The lion's job is to kill the dragon named Thou Shalt. When it has been killed by the lion of self-discovery, all the energy that had been caught up in the dragon is now yours. People in mid-life who are still expecting benefits from being good, or punishment from being bad, are delayed. Their infantile egos are still operating in midlife, and this is not appropriate.

When you come into Jung's second stage, the last half of life, the quest is for the import of the OM that you've heard in the heart chakra, so that it will become the forming and structuring energy of your life, without care for achievement, without care for prestige.

Almost anyone making a transition would have an experience of shedding the old skin. Suppose you have shed the serpent's skin but want to leave some tagged on the end. This is a major problem. It is an anxiety that has to do with what's back there. You have to know enough to cut it off. You have to know what it is that's hanging on: the old skin that is being peeled away gradually, bit by bit, like taking off a bandage without pulling all the hair.

Sri Ramakrishna, talking about this fundamental stage of renunciation—"going into the forest," in the Indian system—speaks of three kinds of renunciation.

The first is gradual renunciation. That's where you know the time is coming, you take advice from your guru or chaplain or whatever, you think it out, make arrangements for the place you're going, and so on. If you are a man, you transfer your dharma to your son. He is the one that now has to carry on the dharma of the family, and you are released from that. Then you are nobody, no longer in caste. It's a real, real quittance.

The second is sudden renunciation. Ramakrishna gives the example of a man who is on his way down to the stream to wash one morning, when he has an argument with his wife. The man says to her, "Now you shut up, or I will go into the forest, become a yogi, and you'll never see me again." She says, "Oh, you would never do that." And he says, "I wouldn't? Watch." And he walks into the forest with his towel on his shoulder. That's sudden renunciation.

Then there is what he calls "monkey renunciation," when a man who has gone away into the forest finds a nice comfortable ashram. He writes back to his family that he has gone to the ashram, and it's going fine. That is not renunciation.

The recommended one is gradual renunciation. That means getting quit of what you can in a decent, organic way. You can even take with you a few little responsibilities, with the understanding that they are terminal—you're not going to add to them. The responsibilities that you add will be those of your own new condition, whatever that may be.

Now in my case, I leave for the forest, as it were—actually, for Hawaii—with three volumes of a book to do, but it's still renunciation: I've cut off my lecturing, and I'm settling in out there with my library and my notes, and I'm just digging in. Renunciation is literally a death and a resurrection. It wasn't easy writing letters to people I'm fond of, people I like working with, and saying I wouldn't be able to go on these lecture trips.

I like Hawaii. It's nice to be in a place where everybody's having a good time. No children are allowed in the building, so all around us are people of about our own age, all still married. It is so nice to be with people still in love with each other after all the rough water of the years past. It's like ships that have come into harbor and are now just floating with all kinds of sea stories.

I work out on a veranda—they call it a "lanai" out there—with my back to the ocean and to what's going on. What's going on is usually a startling bikini walking past. I couldn't write about anything but the Goddess if I were looking in the other direction. So mine is a nice sort of forest to retire to.

"In primitive tribes, we observe that the old people are almost always the guardians of the mysteries and the laws, and it is in these that the cultural heritage of the tribe is expressed."—Jung [42]

In old age, your only relationship to the world is your begging bowl, which in our culture is your bank account. That's what you've already earned, and it has to support this relatively carefree last stage of life. Since I am myself in that stage now, I can tell you that it is the best part of life. It's properly called, in this wonderful language that we have, the "Golden Years." It is a period when everything is coming up and flowering. It is very, very sweet.

...the old in many societies spend a considerable part of their time playing with and taking care of the youngsters, while the parents delve and spin: so that the old are returned to the sphere of eternal things not only within but without. And we may take it also, I should think, that the considerable mutual attraction of the very young and the very old may derive something from their common, secret knowledge that it is they, and not the busy generation between, who are concerned with a poetic play that is eternal and truly wise. [43]

The image of decline in old age is a bit deceptive, because even though your energies are not those of early youth—that was the time of moving into the field of making all the big drives—now you are in the field, and this is the time of the opening flower, the real fulfillment, the bringing forth of what you have prepared yourself to bring forth. It is a wonderful moment. It is not a loss situation, as if you're throwing off something to go down. Not at all. It is a blooming.

"When he comes to weakness—whether he come to weakness through old age or through disease—this person frees himself from these limbs just as a mango, or a fig, or a berry releases itself from its bond; and he hastens again, according to the entrance and place of origin, back to life. As noblemen, policemen, chariot-drivers, village-heads wait with food, drink, and lodgings for a king who is coming, and cry: 'Here he comes! Here he comes!' so indeed do all things wait for him who has this knowledge and cry: 'Here is the Imperishable coming! Here is the Imperishable coming!'"
—Brihadaranyaka Upanishad, 4- 3- 36–37[44]

PEOPLE ask me, "What can we have for rituals?" Well, what do you want to have a ritual for? You should have a ritual for your life. All a ritual does is concentrate your mind on the implications of what you are doing. For instance, the marriage ritual is a meditation on the step you are taking in learning to become a member of a duad, instead of one individual all alone. The ritual enables you to make the transit.

> Ritual introduces you
> to the meaning of what's going on.

> Saying grace before meals
> lets you know that you're about to eat
> something that once was alive.

When eating a meal, realize what you are doing. Hunting peoples thank the animal for having given itself. They feel real gratitude. The main rituals of mature hunting tribes, like those of the Americas, were addressed to the animal. On the Northwest Coast, the principle rites were when the first wave of salmon came in, and they were intended to thank the salmon.

> The life of the animal that you've taken
> is given back when you recognize
> what you've done.

And so, sitting down to eat, realize what you are doing: you are eating a life that has been given so that you might live.

...man, like no other animal, not only knows that he is killing when he kills but also knows that he too will die; and the length of his old age, furthermore, is—like his infancy—a lifetime in itself, as long as the entire span of many a beast.[45]

When I was working on the Gospel of Sri Rama-krishna, I had a lot of meals with the monks. Their grace before meals is the most beautiful invocation. It goes like this: "Brahman is the cosmic, universal, life consciousness energy of which we are all manifestations. Brahman is the sacrifice. Brahman is the food that we are eating. Brahman is the consumer of the sacrifice. Brahman is the ladle that carries the sacrifice to the fire. Brahman is the process of the sacrifice. He who recognizes that all things are Brahman is on the way to realizing Brahman in himself."

The meaning of this grace is that taking food into your system is like putting a libation into a sacrificial fire: the fire of your digestive apparatus consumes what you eat, so eating is the counterpart of a sacrifice.

The communion ritual is an extension of this idea, a motif that came into the world with the dawn of agriculture: "If the seed does not die, there is no plant." It dies as seed and yields to the sprout. Now, since we are composed of spirit and matter—the two substances are what live in us—we need two types of food. The food that nourishes our material part —vegetables, animals, whatever it is we eat—is earthly food, but we must also have spiritual food, nourishment for our spiritual part. And communion, the eating of Christ, is a symbolization of the imbibing of that spiritual nourishment, a concretization of the idea of meditation, But in order to eat anything, it has to be killed, so again we have this notion of the sacrifice.

> You should be willing
> to be eaten also.
> You are food body.

Every ritual is of that order, properly putting your mind in touch with what you really are doing. And so, we should realize that this event here and now: our coming together to help each other in the realization is a beautiful, beautiful ritual.

You can ritualize your entire life that way, and it's extremely helpful to do so. The whole thing of compassion comes in there. What helped me was waking up and thinking of my penny catechism: "to know, to love, to serve God." I don't think of God as up there. I think of God as right here in whatever I'm knowing and loving and serving. "To be happy with Him forever in heaven" means to recognize your own compassion, your own participation in that creature or person you're with. That seems to be the goal of the journey.

The principle ritual in most puberty and initiation rites is a death and resurrection ritual in which your name is changed. You die to the name you had and are resurrected with a new identity.

I once saw a film of the consecration of a group of young men who were becoming monks. They were standing in the aisle of a church, and then they all prostrated themselves, and a great canvas emblazoned with the cross was laid over them. When the canvas was removed, they were monks.

The experience of boys being initiated in Australia and New Guinea is of death. Their eyes are covered, and they hear the bullroarer coming, and they are told that the dragon is coming to consume them. When it is right over their heads and they're about to be eaten, their eyes are uncovered, and now initiated, they see that it's Uncle Charlie with the bullroarer.

In another such rite, described in a book about the Ona of Tierra del Fuego, the boy is in the men's house, where there are these masked forms that he believes to be deities and punishing powers. One of them comes forward, and the boy has to wrestle with him. The man whom he's fighting almost puts the boy down, but then he yields. He lets the boy defeat him and pull off his mask. Then the mask is not simply regarded as a fake. It is both conquered and worshiped, because it represents both the bounding and the bonding power of the society. The boy puts the mask on himself, and he is now that power. What was feared is transformed into what is now supported.

I was very much interested in the work of George Catlin, who did hundreds of paintings of American Indians. He traveled among the Mandan Indians in 1832 and painted a series of pictures depicting their initiation rites. The young men are hung from the ceiling by spikes through their chests and spun around until they collapse. One young man said to him, "Our women suffer, and we must learn to suffer too."

That was, to me, a very interesting observation, because suffering overtakes women. There is nothing they can do to avoid it. When a girl has her first menstruation, she's a woman.

Now the fear of menstrual blood, which is almost biological in the male, is in primitive cultures emphatic. There is a real fear of it that incorporates the whole mystery and power. Consequently, the girl's initiation at that time usually consists of her sitting, isolated, in a little hut, realizing that she is a woman. Next thing she knows, in most societies, she's a mother.

I've been told by some women that the first crash-through of this blood is a shock and a fearful thing. It's a threshold-crossing that you've been pushed across. You don't have to strive for anything. What you have to do is come to know what's happened: appreciate the implications of the biological change that's taken place without effort. After listening to many women, I have had the realization that the woman's characteristic experience is having to endure something, and that the prime requirement is tolerance, the ability to endure.

The man, on the other hand, has to go out to seek the problem. The boy, accordingly, has to be systematically withdrawn from the women and put in the men's camp in order to find his action field. As a man, he will have to endure only moments of great pain and struggle and difficulty with things just out of sight, which is what gets thrown at him in the initiation rites. The boy has to *enact* being a man. The girl has to *realize* that she's a woman. Life overtakes her.

The man never has a comparable experience. That's why many male initiation rites are so violent—so that the man knows for certain he is no longer a little boy. And that's also why a young man has to be disengaged from his mother. In our culture, there are mothers who understand this and assist in the separation. A clinging mother is a terrible weight on the life of a young man. In the primitive cultures, they are definitely separated.

I was just reading of a Hindu rite in Bengal, where the woman's condition is extremely blocked. As a girl, she has to do what her father tells her to do; when she marries, she has to do what her husband tells her to do; when he dies, if she doesn't throw herself on the funeral pyre, she has to do what her oldest son tells her to do. She's never her own boss. Her only strong emotional connections are with her children, and the strongest is with her son.

So, there is this ritual to enable the woman to let her son go. Over a series of years, the family chaplain, the guru, comes and asks her for some valuable thing that she must give him. It starts with some of her jewelry—about the only possessions she has—and then she has to give up certain food that she likes. She has to learn to be quit of that which she values. Then comes the time when her son is no longer a little boy, and by then she has learned how to say that the most precious thing in her life can go.

Have I ever told you about the ritual in Kentucky where I had to give up seven things? It was one of the most interesting group experiences I've ever had. We were a group of about forty-nine people in one of those meetings of some society for the transformation of consciousness. Two couples from the University of Vermont, professors and their wives, had arranged a ritual that we were all going to undertake. We were divided into seven groups of seven and told to spend a day thinking of the seven things without which we'd not want to live: "What are the seven things for which you feel your life is worth living?" Then you were to gather seven little objects, small enough to hold in your hand, which were to represent your seven cherished things, and you were to know which was which.

In the evening we went down a wooded road in the dark to the mouth of a cave. The cave had a wooden door on it which could be opened. In front of the door was a man wearing the mask of a dog: Cerberus at the gate of hell. He put his hand out and said, "Give me that which you least cherish." When you gave him one of the little objects you were holding, he opened the door and allowed you to enter.

Then you proceeded forward through the cave, an enormous place, holding the six remaining things you most cherished. On five further occasions, you were asked to surrender that which you least cherished, until you were left with one object that represented what you treasured most. And you found out what it was, believe me. You really, really did. And the order in which you gave up your treasures was revelatory: you really knew what your order of values was. Then you came to an exit, where there were two people between whom you had to go. But before you could go through that guarded exit, you had to give up that which you most cherished.

I can tell you that ritual worked. All of the participants with whom I've talked had an actual experience of *moska*, "release," when they had given up their last treasure. One damned fool was the exception. He did not give up anything. That's how seriously this ritual was taken. When he was asked to give up something, he just stooped down, picked up a pebble, and handed that over. That's the refusal of the call.

> *...every failure to cope with a life situation must be laid, in the end, to a restriction of consciousness. Wars and temper tantrums are the makeshifts of ignorance; regrets are illuminations come too late.*[46]

The exciting thing to me was the actual experience. It was a feeling of joyous participation. Watching your earlier bondages go really did change your feeling for the treasures you'd given up. It increased your love for them without the tenacity. I was amazed.

THE meditation associated with catastrophes like the end of the world is on this process of coming and going, coming and going, and settling yourself at peace with the fact that things come and go.

> Apocalypse
> does not point to a fiery Armageddon,
> but to our ignorance and complacency
> coming to an end.

I've been feeling that a terrific amount of the anxiety associated with the fear of an impending atomic explosion and the dissolution of the universe is a projection of anxiety coming from a world of people who have never found the center beyond coming and going. If you are at peace with eternity, the blowing up of the universe is perfectly acceptable—just as your own death has to be acceptable. It is going with organic processess. Everything that comes... goes.

> ...*the hero would be no hero if death held for him any terror; the first condition is reconciliation with the grave.*[47]

Chief Seattle, of the Indians that inhabited the Seattle area, wrote a wonderful paper that has to do with putting oneself in tune with the universe. He said, "Why should I lament the disappearance of my people?

All things end, and the white man will find this out also." And this goes for the universe. One can be at peace with that. This doesn't mean that one shouldn't participate in efforts to correct the situation, but underlying the effort to change must be an "at peace." To win a dog sled race is great. To lose is okay too.

The world of human life is now the problem. Guided by the practical judgment of the kings and the instruction of the priests of the dice of divine revelation, the field of consciousness so contracts that the grand lines of the human comedy are lost in a welter of cross-purposes. Men's perspectives become flat, comprehending only the light-reflecting, tangible surfaces of existence. The vista into depth closes over. The significant form of the human agony is lost to view. Society lapses into mistake and disaster. The Little Ego has usurped the judgment seat of the Self.[48]

Let us imagine ourselves for a moment in the lecture hall. ...Above, we see many lights. Each bulb is separate from the others, and we may think of them, accordingly, as separate from each other.
...just as each bulb seen aloft is a vehicle of light, so each of us below is a vehicle of consciousness. But the important thing about a bulb is the quality of its light. Likewise, the important thing about each of us is the quality of his consciousness. And although each may tend to identify himself mainly with his separate body and its frailties, it is possible also to regard one's body as a mere vehicle of consciousness and to think then of consciousness as the one presence here made manifest through us all.[49]

> If the body is a light bulb, and it burns out,
> does that mean there's no more electricity?
> The source of energy remains.

We can discard the body and go on.
We are the source.

"For that which is born, death is certain, and for that which is dead, birth is certain. You should not grieve over the unavoidable.... The Supreme Self which dwells in all bodies, can never be slain.... Weapons cut it not; fire burns it not; water wets it not; the wind does not wither it. Eternal, universal, unchanging, immovable, the Self is the same forever. ...Dwelling in all bodies, the Self can never be slain. Therefore you should not grieve for any creature."—Bhagavad Gita[50]

"All things are in process, rising and returning. Plants come to blossom, but only to return to the root. Returning to the root is like seeking tranquility. Seeking tranquility is like moving toward destiny. To move toward destiny is like eternity. To know eternity is enlightenment, and not to recognize eternity brings disorder and evil. Knowing eternity makes one comprehensive; comprehension makes one broadminded; breadth of vision brings nobility; nobility is like heaven."—Lao-tse[51]

We go down into death for refreshment.

"Nothing retains its own form; but Nature, the greater renewer, ever makes up forms from forms. Be sure there's nothing perishes in the whole universe; it does but vary and renew its form."—Ovid[52]

An Aztec prayer to be said at the deathbed... "Dear Child! Thou hast passed through and survived the labors of this life. Now it hath pleased our Lord to carry thee away. For we do not enjoy this world everlastingly, only briefly; our life is like the warming of oneself in the sun.[53]

How one comes to accept that life follows death is an individual problem. There are a lot of meditation disciplines that open one to the experience of death, the acceptance of death. It is a motif that is absolutely universal in initiations. There is always a death aspect and a birth after it.

> Death and begetting
> come at the same time.

Only birth can conquer death—the birth, not of the old thing again, but of something new. Within the soul, within the body social, there must be—if we are to experience long survival—a continuous "recurrence of birth" (palingenesia) to nullify the unremitting recurrences of death.[54] For it is by means of our own victories, if we are not regenerated, that the work of Nemesis is wrought: doom breaks from the shell of our very virtue. Peace then is a snare; war is a snare; change is a snare; permanence a snare. When our day is come for the victory of death, death closes in; there is nothing we can do, except be crucified and resurrected; dismembered totally, and then reborn.[55]

Sometimes the death is, as it were, enacted. In primitive puberty rites, there is often an enactment of dying or the young person thinks he's about to be killed and actually experiences a going into death. I know of a number of examples in contemporary life of people who have been in a blocked situation and then have actually experienced death.

One case I know was a woman caught in an automobile accident where two trucks collided with her in the middle, and she thought she was dead. When she came out of it, the whole life that she had been living just dropped off, and she had an entirely new life. So it is a valid psychological theme, this one of death out of which life comes.

Among primitive hunting people, where the men continually kill animals, this killing of the animals is the principle sacrifice, and among those people typically we have no human sacrifices. But in early planting cultures, there is almost a fury of sacrifice, sacrifices of all kinds, and it's in those cultures that we have human sacrifice.

Only the best are sacrificed.

Being sacrificed is a way to go home.

"He who loses his life shall find it."

Generally, the principle sacrifice is of a major food animal. For instance, in Southeast Asia, it's the pig; in Europe, principally, it's the bull. Both of these animals are symbolic of the moon. The tusks of the pig are the crescents of the moon, with the black face between; the horns of the bull, the same. The moon is that which dies and is resurrected, dies and is resurrected. The bull represents, in a way, the death of the moon out of which a new life can come.

Snake and moon both die to the old,
shed their shadow to be reborn.

In Rome, suicide was a noble act. When one was about to be captured, which would mean living a disgraceful life, there was suicide, a practice that went on among the Celts too. There is a Hellenistic picture of a Celt killing himself and his wife as they're about to be captured.

In Japan, the highest example of ceremonial suicide is *hara-kiri*, an interesting and subtle ritual act. A man who has conspicuously failed in the performance of his duty, which he places above his personal wish, commits *hara-kiri*, for it is the only thing that can redeem him from the disgrace. The man who is to commit *hara-kiri* kneels in the center of a tatami mat, the four corners of which are marked off by objects —like Matthew, Mark, Luke, and John around Christ: the motif of the center and the four points. He inserts his sword, the symbol of his nobility and honor, into the right side of his belly, and carries it across and down. He must fall face forward. It is an extremely painful way to kill yourself. You can't just stab and go out. It is a deliberate act, and a matter of honor that you experience the whole thing. In the woman's counter-part of *hara-kiri*, she cuts her jugular vein—a different act, but the sense is the same.

An Indian aristocrat, whose sword is his honor, can behead himself. You can't practice this one either. The way it's done, according to the illustrations, is you bend down a pliant sapling, attach a rope to it, put the rope around your head, bend over, take your sword, and cut off your head. The farther the tree pitches your head, the greater the merit you've gained by the act. You are immediately translated to wherever the merit has brought you, and your friends 'round about know what has happened. This type of suicide has high dignity and belongs to the ritual practice of the community.

I think the idea of life after death is a bad idea. It distracts you from appreciating the uniqueness of the here and now, the moment you are living. For example, if you think that when you die your parents will be there and you'll live with them forever, you may no longer appreciate the significant moments that you share with them on earth.

Every moment is utterly unique and will not be continued in eternity. This fact gives life its poignancy and should concentrate your attention on what you are experiencing now. I think that's washed out a bit by the notion that everyone will be happy in heaven. You had better be happy here, now. You'd better experience the eternal here and now.. Being "happy with Him forever in heaven" means that while you are here on earth you should be happy: that is to say, your life should be identified with the divine power, the eternal power in all life. If you concretize the symbol of heaven, the whole situation disintegrates. You think, for example, that eternity is there, and your life is here. You believe that God, the source of energy, is there, and you are here, and He may come into your life or He may not. No, no—that source of eternal energy is here, in you, now.

That is the essence of Gnosticism, Buddha consciousness, and so forth. St. Paul got close to the idea when he said, "I live now, not I, but Christ in me." I once made this observation in a lecture, and a priest in attendance said, "That's blasphemy."—an example of the church not conceding the very sense of the symbol.

On the other hand, since the function of the heaven image is to help you to die, to yield to where nature's taking you rather than resist, I think you would tell a Christian child who is going to die that he is going to go to heaven.

> The resistance to death
> has to do with not knowing
> where you're going when you die.

In one of the sutras, the Buddha is asked how one person helps another face death. He responds: "Suppose a house caught fire, and in the house was a father with three little children, and the children were afraid of the flames, but they wouldn't go outside. The father says, 'Now, look, outside we have a darling little goat cart. The goats are all waiting for you, so let's go out and get in the cart.'" That is to say, you put something out past the flames for the person who is not able to experience anything else. This approach is a convenient means of bringing about a desirable and necessary act that the person would otherwise be incapable of performing.

When you support someone who is dying, you are helping that person to identify with the consciousness that is going to disengage from the body. We disengage from various things all of our lives. Finally, we identify with consciousness and disengage from our bodies.

> In Buddhism,
> the central thought is
> compassion without attachment.

And so, the death of one for whom you feel compassion should't be an affliction. Your attachment is the temporal aspect of the relationship; your compassion is the eternal aspect. Hence, you can reconcile yourself to feelings of loss by identifying with that which is not lost when all is lost: namely, the consciousness that informs the body and all things. This yielding back into undifferentiated consciousness is the return, and that is as far as you can think, as much as you can know. The rest is transcendent of all conscious knowledge.

Coming
into Awareness

*T*HE *first aphorism of Patanjali's classic
handbook of yoga supplies the key to the entire work:
"Yoga consists in the intentional stopping
of the spontaneous activity of the mind-stuff."*[56]
*...Any person unused to meditation, desiring to fix in
his mind a single image or thought, will find within seconds
that he is already entertaining associated thoughts. The un-
trained mind will not stand still, and yoga is the intentional
stopping of its movement.*

*It may be asked, why should anyone wish to bring about
such a state?*

*The mind is likened, in reply, to the surface of a pond
rippled by a wind.... The idea of yoga is to cause that wind to
subside and let the waters return to rest. For when a wind
blows and waters stir, the waves break and distort both the
light and its reflections, so that all that can be seen are collid-
ing broken forms. Not until the waters will have been stilled,
cleansed of stirred-up sediment and made mirror-bright, will
the one reflected image appear that on the rippling waves had
been broken; that of the clouds and pure sky above, the trees
along the shore, and down deep in the still, pure water itself,
the sandy bottom and the fish. Then alone will that single
image be known of which the wave-borne reflections are but
fragments and distortions. And this single image can be
likened to that of the Self realized in yoga. It is the Ultimate
—the Form of forms—of which the phenomena of this world
are but imperfectly seen, ephemeral distortions: the God-form,*

*the Buddha-form, which is truly our own Knowledge-form,
and with which it is the goal of yoga to unite us.*[57]

In kundalini yoga, largely through the exercise of
meditation and breath control, called *pranayama*—
breathing in through one nostril for a certain number
of counts, holding the breath, filling the body with the
prana, the breath, then breathing out for a number of
counts, holding briefly, breathing in through the other
nostril, and so forth—one gradually stills the whole
psyche, calms the waters, as it were.

There is a notion that breath and emotion are
linked. When you are shocked, your breathing changes.
When you are full of rage or passion of any kind, your
breathing changes. When you are at rest, your breathing changes. So the goal here is to make your breathing
regular, to still and calm the mind. And at the same
time there is a meditation that activates the Kundalini
serpent and starts her up the spine.

*[Kundalini]...the figure of a coiled female serpent—a
serpent goddess not of "gross" but of "subtle" substance—
which is to be thought of as residing in a torpid, slumbering
state in a subtle center, the first of the seven, near the base of
the spine: the aim of the yoga then being to rouse this
serpent, lift her head, and bring her up a subtle nerve or
channel of the spine to the so-called "thousand-petaled lotus"
(sahasrara) at the crown of the head....She, rising from the
lowest to the highest lotus center, will pass through and wake
the five between, and with each waking the psychology and
personality of the practitioner will be altogether and
fundamentally transformed.*[58]

The word *chakra* means "wheel." *Chakras* are also
called *padmas*, which means "lotuses." There are seven:
three associated with the pelvic area, three with the

head, and one in between—the heart chakra—in that great cavity of all the pulses: the pulsation of the heart and the pulsation of the breath.

Chakra I, Muladhara, *the "Root Support," is located at the base of the spine. The world view is of uninspired materialism, governed by 'hard facts'...and the psychology, adequately described in behavioristic terms, is reactive, not active. There is on this plane no zeal for life, no explicit impulse to expand. There is simply a lethargic avidity in hanging on to existence; and it is this grim grip that must finally be broken so that the spirit may be quit of its dull zeal simply to be....*

The first task of the yogi, then, must be to break at this level the cold dragon grip of his own spiritual lethargy and release the jewel-maid, his own shakti, for ascent to those higher spheres where she will become his spiritual teacher and guide to the bliss of an immortal life beyond sleep.[59]

Chakra II, Svadhisthana, *"Her Special Abode," is at the level of the genitals. When the Kundalini is active at this level, the whole aim of life is in sex. Not only is every thought and act sexually motivated, either as a means toward sexual ends or as a compensating sublimation of frustrated sexual zeal, but everything seen and heard is interpreted compulsively, both consciously and unconsciously, as symbolic of sexual themes. Psychic energy, that is to say, has the character here of the Freudian libido. Myths, deities, and religious rites are understood and experienced in sexual terms.*[60]

Chakra III, Manipura, *"City of the Shining Jewel," is located at the level of the navel. Here the energy turns to violence and its aim is to consume, to master, to turn the world into oneself and one's own. The appropriate Occidental psychology would be the Adlerian of the "will to power": for now even sex becomes an occasion, not of erotic experience,* *but of achievement, conquest, self-reassurance, and frequently, also, revenge.*[61]

The function of Chakra III is organizing your life, establishing a family, building a business, learning how to master the world in terms appropriate to your condition and place. Self maintenance, family maintenance. society maintenance, world maintenance —but maintenance in the sense of transformation: life is maintained, not in a petrified condition, but in a growth condition, as is a tree by the gardener that cultivates it.

All three of these lower chakras are of the modes of man's living in the world in his naive state, outward turned: the modes of the lovers, the fighters, the builders, the accomplishers. Joys and sorrows on these levels are functions of achievements in the world "out there," what people think of one, what has been gained, what lost.[62]

These three chakras are of functions that we share with the other animals. They are also clinging to life, begetting, building nests, making their way. Popular religion works on these levels, and the individual living on these levels is ego-oriented and his action must be controlled by social law.

...a religion operating only on these levels, having little or nothing to do with the fostering of inward, mystical realizations, would hardly merit the name of religion at all. It would be little more than an adjunct to police authority, offering in addition to ethical rules and advice intangible consolations for life's losses and a promise of future rewards for social duties fulfilled.[63]

Chakra IV, *Anahata*, meaning "not hit," is at the level of the heart. It is the beginning of the religious life, the awakening where the new life begins, and its name refers to the sound that is not made by any two things striking together. All the sounds that we hear are made by two things striking together. What would the sound be that is not made by two things striking together? It is the sound of the energy of which universe is a manifestation. It is, therefore, antecedent to things.

The heart chakra, then, is the opening of the spiritual dimension: all is metaphoric of the mystery. Once you have got that point of all being metaphoric of the mystery, then these lower powers become spiritualized. The very doing of the things of the first three chakras become the realizations of Chakras V, VI, and VII.

> When you reach the upper chakras,
> you don't do without the first three:
> survival, sex, power.
>
> You don't destroy
> the first three floors of a building
> when you get to the fourth.

Chakra V, called *Vishuddha*, "Purified," is at the level of the larynx. This is the chakra of spiritual effort to hold back the animal system from which the energies come. One has gone through the lower chakras to get to here, but the pelvic chakras have not been rejected. They now have to be turned to a spiritual, rather than a merely physical, aim. Chakra V is commonly referred to by Tibetan images of deities standing on prostrate forms, putting down the merely physical with weapons and ferocity: the ferocity with which you have to handle yourself.

Chakra VI, *Ajna*, the lotus of "Command," located between the eyebrows, is what we would call the chakra of heaven, the highest chakra in the world of incarnate forms. The forms of the pharaohs from Egypt show the Uraeus Serpent coming out of this point between the brows. When the Kundalini has reached this point, one beholds God. Any god you have been meditating on or have been taught to revere is the god that will be seen here. This is the highest obstacle for the complete yogi. As Ramakrishna says, "One is tempted to stay there tasting the juice." It is so sweet, so blissful.

> On the brink of illumination,
> the old ways are very seductive
> and liable to pull you back.

The Sufis have a wonderful image connected with Chakra VI. This is the story told by Hallaj: One night a moth sees a lamp, a burning flame enclosed in glass. It spends the whole night bumping against the glass, trying to become one with the flame. In the morning it returns to its friends and tells them of the beautiful thing it has seen. They say, "You don't look the better for it." This is the condition of the yogi trying to break through. So it goes back the next night and, somehow or other, gets through. For an eternal instant it achieves its goal: it becomes the flame—*tat tvam asi*—"thou art that." And so, here is the subject and here is the object—the Soul and God—between is a pane of glass. Remove the pane and there is neither subject nor object, because to have an object you have to have a subject.

The final barrier to enlightenment is the barrier that prevents you from becoming God. The pane of glass is a way of speaking about the dividing factor. Removing the glass suggests the annihilation of the veil of ignorance that keeps you from knowing God. Beholding God—God with characteristics—is the final whisp of ignorance. At this level you have to have a symbol, an experience because you are still holding the last whisp of you. I am beholding God. That's the final barrier.

It is so sweet that one is reluctant to yield, but the ultimate yielding is the yielding of your own being. If you're going to hang onto your soul, you can't become one with God. You can't even become one with your spouse. This is what has to be given up. I hear OM. I know God is ubiquitous. Divine energy is all around me. It is here. It is here. It is here.

When you come to fulfillment, you have come to that high point. The god's name doesn't matter, they are all included. The different gods are personifications of aspects of the total functioning. The ultimate thing is going past gods. Meister Eckhart said, "The ultimate leave-taking is the leaving of God for God."[64] That means leaving the folk idea of God—the ecclesiastical idea of God, what you've been taught of God—for that transcendent reference of which God is the metaphor. Where are you between two thoughts? Where is God between two Gods?

It's a simple idea, yet we are so used to being taught something else that the words tend to block us instead of letting us through. Leaving God for God is, for me, a very vivid statement. Indian philosophy has no problem with this concept. When the Kundalini reaches Chakra VI, you see God: "Brahman with characteristics." At Chakra VII, you go past God and are in the transcendent: "Brahman without characteristics."

Chakra VII, *Sahasrara*, "Thousand Petalled," is the lotus at the crown of the head. At this chakra there is no person to be conscious of God. There is only undifferentiated consciousness: the silence. When you hit Chakra VII, you are inert. It is a catatonic knockout, you might say, and you are reduced simply to a thing.

Now as I see it, if you come back down to the heart, to Chakra IV, where spiritual life begins, subject and object are together. Chakra I corresponds to VII. The inertia from Chakra I sets in when you have hit Chakra VII. Chakra II corresponds to VI. Chakra III corresponds to V. You are then able to take the war energy from Chakra III and practice self control in Chakra V. So you can bend things at Chakra IV.

For example, through the experiences of Chakra II, if they are of love, you are really experiencing the grace of God in Chakra VI. You transmute the lust energy of Chakra II into love. If there has been no experience of the discipline of Chakra V, you'll never get an inkling of what it is you are to be experiencing through the physical. If in your physical love, you can realize that what you are touching is the grace of the divine in its proper form for you, this is a translation of the carnal adventure into the spiritual, without the loss of the carnal. The two are together. You are then beholding the god as in Chakra VI and experiencing the beloved as a manifestation of that divine power, that love which informs the world.

In the courtly love tradition, the woman had to test the man by holding him off until she was sure that it was not lust that was approaching her, but love, the gentle heart. That is the whole sense of courtly love. The same theme is later represented in Dante's *Divine Comedy*, where his love for Beatrice brings him to the throne of God. In his wonderful book of poems called *La Vita Nuova, "The New Life,"* Dante describes how he looks at her, not with the eye of Chakra II, but with that of Chakra VI, as a manifestation of God's love, and that carries him through the whole thing.

My wonderful friend, Heinrich Zimmer, my final guru, often said, "The best things cannot be told." That is to say, you can't talk about that which lies beyond the reach of words.

The second best are misunderstood, because they are your statements about that which cannot be told. They are misunderstood because the vocabulary of symbols that you have to use are thought to be references to historical events.

The third best is conversation, political life, economics, and all that. And that's what we are usually dealing with: the first three chakras.

Zimmer loved to recount an amusing animal-fable from India. It tells of a tigress, pregnant and starving, who comes upon a little flock of goats and pounces on them with such energy that she brings about the birth of her little one and her own death.

The goats scatter, and when they come back to their grazing place, they find this just-born tiger and its dead mother. Having strong parental instincts, they adopt the tiger, and it grows up thinking it's a goat. It learns to bleat. It learns to eat grass. And since grass doesn't nourish it very well, it grows up to become a pretty miserable specimen of its species.

When the young tiger reaches adolescence, a large male tiger pounces on the flock, and the goats scatter. But this little fellow is a tiger, so he stands there. The big one looks at him in amazement and says, "Are you living here with these goats?" "Maaaaaa," says the little tiger. Well, the old tiger is mortified, something like a father who comes home and finds his son with long hair. He swats him back and forth a couple of times, and the little thing just responds with these silly bleats and begins nibbling grass in embarrassment. So the big tiger brings him to a still pond.

Now, still water is a favorite Indian image to symbolize the idea of yoga. The first aphorism of yoga is: "Yoga is the intentional stopping of the spontaneous activity of the mind-stuff." Our minds, which are in continual flux, are likened to the surface of a pond that's blown by a wind. So the forms that we see, those of our own lives and the world around us, are simply flashing images that come and go in the field of time, but beneath all of them is the substantial form of forms. Bring the pond to a standstill, have the wind withdraw and the waters clear, and you'll see, in stasis, the perfect image beneath all of these changing forms.

So this little fellow looks into the pond and sees his own face for the first time. The big tiger puts his face over and says, "You see, you've got a face like mine. You're not a goat. You're a tiger like me. Be like me."

Now that's guru stuff: I'll give you my picture to wear, be like me. It's the opposite to the individual way.

So the little one is getting that message; he's picked up and taken to the tiger's den, where there are the remains of a recently slaughtered gazelle. Taking a chunk of this bloody stuff, the big tiger says, "Open your face." The little one backs away, "I'm a vegetarian." "None of that nonsense," says the big fellow, and he shoves a piece of meat down the little one's throat. He gags on it. The text says, "As all do on true doctrine."

But gagging on the true doctrine, he's nevertheless getting it into his blood, into his nerves; it's his proper food. It touches his proper nature. Spontaneously, he gives a tiger stretch, the first one. A little tiger roar comes out—Tiger Roar 101. The big one says, "There. Now you've got it. Now we go into the forest and eat tiger food."

118

> Vegetarianism
> is the first turning away from life,
> because life lives on lives.
> Vegetarians are just eating
> something that can't run away.

Now, of course, the moral is that we are all tigers living here as goats. The right hand path, the sociological department, is interested in cultivating our goat-nature. Mythology, properly understood as metaphor, will guide you to the recognition of your tiger face. But then how are you going to live with these goats?

Well, Jesus had something to say about this problem. In Matthew 7 he said, "Do not cast your pearls before swine, or they will trample them under their feet and turn and tear you."

> The function
> of the orthodox community
> is to torture the mystic to death:
> his goal.

You wear the outer garment of the law, behave as everyone else and wear the inner garment of the mystic way. Jesus also said that when you pray, you should go into your own room and close the door. When you go out, brush your hair. Don't let them know. Otherwise, you'll be a kook, something phony.

So that has to do with not letting people know where you are. But then comes the second problem: how do you live with these people? Do you know the answer? You know that they are all tigers. And you live with that aspect of their nature, and perhaps in your art you can let them know that they are tigers.

And that's the revelation then. And so this brings us to the final formula of the Bodhisattva way, the way of the one who is grounded in eternity and moving in the field of time. The field of time is the field of sorrow. "All life is sorrowful." And it is. If you try to correct the sorrows, all you do is shift them somewhere else. Life is sorrowful. How do you live with that? You realize the eternal within yourself. You disengage, and yet, reengage. You—and here's the beautiful formula—"participate with joy in the sorrows of the world." You play the game. It hurts, but you know that you have found the place that is transcendent of injury and fulfillments. You are there, and that's it.

I haven't kept up with psychology since the death of Jung, but I'd say that Jung was such a person: one grounded in eternity and moving in the field of time. Jean and I had tea for an hour-and-a-half with Dr. and Mrs. Jung at Bollingen, his place at Lake Zurich. It was a lovely occasion. Since he was editing some of the German posthumata of Zimmer and I had done my work on the English, we had no trouble saying hello and enjoyng things together without any anxiety of understanding. When we were about to leave Jung said, "So, you're going to India. Well, let me tell you the meaning of OM.

"When I was in Africa a group of us went for a little hike. Presently, we knew we were lost. Then we looked around and saw all these boys with things in their noses, standing on one leg, supporting themselves with spears. Nobody knew how to talk to anybody else. We had no knowledge of their language. It was a tense moment. We all just sat down and kept looking at each other. When everybody felt that everything was okay —"it's okay, these are good people, they're perfectly okay"— what do I hear? 'OM...OM...OM...'

"Then, the next year I was in India with a group of scientists, and if there's one variety of the human species that is not susceptible to awe, this is it. We went up to Darjeeling, to Tiger Hill, which is a wonderful experience. You are awakened early in the morning about a half hour before sunrise and driven in the chilly morning air to a lofty ridge. And it's dark. When the sun rises, you see before you millions of square miles of Himalayan peaks breaking into rainbow colors. What did I hear from the scientists? 'OM...OM...OM...' OM is the sound nature makes when it's pleased with itself."

That's an example of the kind of playful conversation that we had. He was a beautiful man, and Jean said that he had beautiful eyes.

Jung found out in 1909 that myth and dream were linked, but it has been well known in India forever. It is implicit in the syllable OM, or A-U-M.

According to the Mandukya Upanishad, the world of the state of waking consciousness is to be identified with the letter A of the syllable AUM; that of dream consciousness (heaven and hell, that is to say) with the letter U; and deep sleep (the state of the mystical union of the knower and the known, God and his world, brooding the seeds and energies of creation: which is the state symbolized in the center of the mandala) with M.[65] The soul is to be propelled both by and from this syllable AUM into the silence beyond and all around it: the silence out of which it rises and back into which it goes when pronounced—slowly and rhythmically ...as AUM—AUM—AUM.[66]

If you want to hear AUM, just cover your ears and you'll hear it. Of course, what you are hearing is the blood in the capillaries, but it's AUM: *Ah*—waking consciousness; *ou*—dream consciousness; and then, *mmm*—the realm of deep, dreamless sleep. AUM is the sound of the radiance of God. This is the most mysterious and important thing to understand, but once you get the idea, it's very simple.

"The dream is a little hidden door in the innermost secret recesses of the soul, opening into that cosmic night which was psyche long before there was any ego-consciousness, and which will remain psyche no matter how far our ego-consciousness may extend. For all ego-consciousness is isolated: because it separates and discriminates, it knows only particulars, and it sees only what can be related to the ego. Its essence is limitation, even though it reach to the farthest nebulae among the stars. All consciousness separates; but in dreams we put on the likeness of that more universal, truer, more eternal man dwelling in the darkness of primordial night. There he is still the whole, and the whole is in him, indistinguishable from nature and bare of all egohood.

"It is from these all-uniting depths that the dream arises, be it never so childish, grotesque, or immoral. So flowerlike is it in its candor and veracity that it makes us blush for the deceitfulness of our lives."—Jung[67]

The secret of dreams is that subject and object are the same. The object is self-luminous, fluent in form, multivalent in its meanings. It's your dream, the manifestation of your will, and yet you are surprised by it. This is the relationship of ego-consciousness to the unconscious. Ego-consciousness has to learn about the unconscious, and dreams are the vocabulary of the unconscious speaking to the conscious mind. Yet, in dreams and in visions, subject and object are the same.

Dream, vision, God—God is a luminous vision. The image of God is equivalent to the dream vision. So your God is an aspect of yourself, just as your dream image is. That's what is meant by the Hindu saying, *nādevo devam arcayet,* "by none but a god shall a god be worshiped." Your god is a manifestation of your own level of consciousness. All of the heavens and all of the hells are within you. This understanding is just taken for granted in India, so we are in the realm of myth.

Write down your dreams.
They are your myths.

Now, this consciousness is unconscious, but the body is conscious; there is consciousness still there. The heart is beating, the blood is running through the body. If you are cold you will pull the blanket up over you; if you are hot you will push the blanket down. I recall a cartoon in a magazine of a husband and wife in bed. He has all the covers over him, and he's dreaming about watching a hula dancer on a South Sea isle. She's freezing and thinks of herself in an Eskimo igloo. The body is conscious.

The point is that consciousness itself is below this level of darkness, beyond dream consciousness. In one of the Upanishads there is a saying: "We go into that Brahman world every night, but, alas, we are asleep." The goal of yoga is to go into that realm awake. If you do, you will have arrived at pure, unmitigated, undifferentiated consciousness. Not consciousness of any thing, because you are not on levels A or U, but consciousness per se. Since all of our words relate either to things or to a relationship of things—whether things of waking or visions of dream—there are no words for this experience. All that can be said about it is silence.

Silence is the proper vocabulary of this realization. The Buddha is called *Shakyamuni*. The word *muni* means "the silent one," and Shakya is his family name, so he is the silent one of the Shakya clan. This is why Zimmer said that the best things can't be told—there are no words for this realization. And when you utter words in order to refer the mind to it, the danger is that the words will trap you and you won't go through. So, for anyone lecturing, there's a not very comfortable saying: "He who speaks, does not know. He who knows, does not speak." That's the final word.

The point is that this AUM heard in silence informs all things. All things are manifestations of it. Now you are inward turned. The secret to having a spiritual life as you move in the world is to hear the AUM in all things all the time. If you do, everything is transformed. You no longer have to go anywhere to find your fulfillment and achievement and the treasure that you seek. It is here. It is everywhere.

Clearly the occurrence of such visions over the whole in-habited earth requires no explanation in terms either of racial or of cultural diffusion. The problem is, rather, psychological: of that depth of the unconscious where, to quote the words of C. G. Jung, "man is no longer a distinct indivi-dual, but his mind widens out and merges into the mind of mankind— not the conscious mind, but the unconscious mind of mankind, where we are all the same."[68]

*N*OW *in every human being there is a built-in human instinct system, without which we should not even come to birth. But each of us has also been educated to a specific local culture system....We are taught to respond to certain signals positively, to others negatively or with fear; and most of these signals taught are not of the natural, but of some local social order. They are socially specific. Yet the impulses that they activate and control are of nature, biology, and instinct.*[69]

In a mature life you're hanging onto life, your erotic relationships are in play and established, and you have found a way to maintain yourself. I will give you an example of how these various energies work against each other. There's one male fish that is normally colored in such a way that the upper part of its body is dark and the lower part is light. That's the usual coloring of fish, because when you are below looking up into the light, the fish is relatively invisible, and when you are above looking down into the dark, it's also camouflaged. But when this particular fish is in love, his color shifts so that he'll be visible. This puts him in danger, you see, and it seems to me symbolic of this love thing. You give up self-protection when this other comes along and you are seized with erotic compulsion.

It's a very amusing exchange. When the female fish goes by, a dance takes place. There is something about his coloration that makes her give a little move, and then that move triggers his response. If any one of the little moves is missed, the dance ends and that choreography is finished. But if they can go through the whole choreography, then something happens.

There was a beautiful movie of three whales: two bulls and a cow. A little job of nature was going to be done for the cow. She was ready. It was one of the most impressive and moving things to see the cooperation of these three animals. They were swimming, the three of them plowing along, and when she was ready to receive one of them, she slowed down. The one on the right was supporting her and, my god, like a rainbow this penis comes curving over the body of this enormous animals. It was very moving and awesome.

When animals get involved with something that comes pushing from inside like that, there are elaborate ritual relationships. One can say that ritual gets going when the species principle begins operating in individuals. It is a commitment of the individual to whatever might be the intention of nature or the society given the circumstances. But how is it that the second bull, who is not involved in the act itself, can participate in this? This to me is something way out. There was absolutely no sense of competition. This was cooperation. I've heard that now that boats are taking out tourists to look at the whales, the whales are moving out beyond Catalina Island. The crowds can ruin anything.

I was watching a flock of birds the other day. The rhythm of their flight is something to see. They all seem to know just when they are going to turn, where they are going, and what's up now. How does this happen? That's participating in a transpersonal rhythm of some kind.

I recall once having seen one of those beautiful Disney nature films, of a sea turtle laying her eggs in the sand, some thirty feet or so from the water. A number of days later, out of the sand there came a little multitude of tiny just-born turtles, each about as big as a nickel; and without an instant's hesitation they all started for the sea. No hunting around. No trial-and-error. No asking, "Now what would be a reasonable place for me to head for first?" Not a single one of those little things went the wrong way, fumbling first into the bushes, and there saying, "Oh!" and turning around, thinking, "I'm made for something better than this!" No, indeed! They went directly as their mother must have known they all would go: mother turtle, or Mother Nature. A flock of seagulls, meanwhile, having screamed the news to each other, came zooming like dive bombers down on those little nickels that were making for the water. The turtles knew perfectly well that that was where they had to get, and they were going as fast as their very little legs could push them: the legs, by the way, already knowing just how to push. No training or experimenting has been necessary. The legs knew what to do, and the little eyes knew that what they were seeing out in front of them was where they were going. The whole system was in perfect operation, with the whole fleet of tiny tanks heading clumsily, yet as fast as they could, for the sea: and then... Well now, one surely would have thought that for such little things those great big waves might have seemed threatening. But no! They went right on into the water and already knew how to swim. And as soon as they were there, of course, the fish began coming at them. Life is tough![70]

The Bushmen in South Africa have very pitiful little bows that don't have a shooting distance beyond twenty yards or so, but they also have a deadly poison that they put on the points of these little arrows. The Bushmen's counterpart to the American Indian's buffalo would be the eland: a big, beautiful type of gazelle. A Bushman has to hypnotize an eland to get close enough to send his arrow. The eland will live for another day in great pain while the poison kills it, and the hunter has to identify himself with the animal and observe certain taboos, and the way he behaves actually influences the death of the animal.

The Hopi Snake Dance relates to this. It's a strange and wonderful ritual, where the dancers hold snakes in their mouths and stroke them with feathers as they dance. I saw a film about the snake worshipping, or snake using, people in the mountains of, I think it was, Georgia or Tennessee. These people have ceremonies in which they toss a tangle of rattlesnakes back and forth. The participants believe that if they are "in the Christ" they won't be bitten. They get themselves into a psychological state that the animals somehow recognize. But in the film, the leader of this particular ceremony is bitten. He says he had a feeling that his consciousness "slipped," as it were, so he won't allow anybody to cure him, and he dies.

Living as I have in New York City, with no real relationship to animals—except when I was a kid out in the country—I never could understand such things. So it's amazing to me to hear stories of what can take place between a human being and a wild animal, when these symbolic ideas of sacrifice and compassion are actually worked out in action.

> How can city people
> call upon animal powers
> if they know nothing about animals?

In Hawaii, I love to watch birds in palm trees. They don't consciously know that palm leaves will go down when they light on them. But when some little bird lands on a leaf that goes down, the bird knows immediately how to catch itself. It's fantastic. What kind of consciousness is that?

I remember when I was a kid walking through the woods and came upon a barbed wire fence with a tree leaning up against it. The tree had incorporated the barbed wire, had very neatly taken it into itself. You cannot tell me there isn't consciousness there. How far down the line does that go?

In the nineteenth century, when systematic vivisection was beginning to be practiced, the animals being used didn't matter. Animals did not have consciousness. Their reactions were thought to be just stimulus responses of a mechanistic organism. How far can you push that way of reading life? Can you bring it right up into human beings? Are we also just mechanistic organisms? That's behavioristic psychology.

The other extreme is what you get with the Hindu perspective of the ubiquity of Atman and Brahman: all things are living things.

> Hindu meditations are intended
> to put you in accord with Nature.
>
> When you are in accord,
> all the boons come.

The ego that relates to the other as to a "Thou" is different from the ego that's relating to an "It." You

130

can turn anything into a Thou, so the whole world is a Thou. That's what the mystical experience is supposed to be. As soon as anything is an It, you have duality. I-Thou is not a duality. It is the nondual realization.

Working with that realization, the whole world is then radiant of life and joy. Finding everything a Thou and realizing it's life is the extreme statement of the implication of all of these religious meditations. That's the perspective that the mechanistic scientists resist.

When I lecture around, it's funny the negative reaction I get from some scientists and Anglo-Saxon philosophers who object to my use of the word "consciousness" for what they would term "energy." I have come more and more to think that these two words are two ways of saying the same thing, two aspects of a single thrust. There's an implicit tendency in consciousness to differentiation and movement, and it strikes me that perhaps the energy we see is consciousness. In the biological sphere at least, energy seems to be associated with consciousness, almost to the point of identity.

I think there are three states of being. One is the innocent expression of Nature. Another is when you pause, analyze, think about it. When you do, Nature is not just living; and while you are analyzing, your nature isn't pushing you. Then, having analyzed, there comes a state in which you're able to live as Nature again, but with more competence, more control, more flexibility.

I am more and more convinced that there is a plane of consciousness that we are all sharing, and that the brain is a limiting machine that pulls it in. It is possible to sink back, lose this definition, and participate in that plane of consciousness. How else do you explain extrasensory perception? And since time is a form of sensibility—meaning, that which is going to happen has already happened in a certain sense—you cannot say that premonitions are coincidences. They are not. They happen too often to be attributed to chance.

I've had such experiences on enough occasions to attest to that: meeting somebody, having a kind of "click," and knowing that you are going to do something important together that will be a major feature in your lives. I mean, when you meet people who are going to be of deep significance in your life, knowing that it's going to happen is somehow right there in the first meeting. It's a very mysterious business.

Sometimes you can feel you've missed the message and gotten off the wave. I have had the feeling that I've missed it, that I should have talked to that person next to me because that's why they were sitting there. But then there are other times when you wonder how the hell a particular person ever got in on your program.

You can get distracted by the desire for psychic powers. Whether you have psychic powers or not, you still face the problem of a life destiny and a life tragedy. I feel that, with the academic life, I have gone on my life journey in a shallow shell. My confession would be that I'm a thinking-intuition type, short in both the feeling side and the sensation side. Okay, that's the boat I have, and that's the one I'm using. My sensations and feelings are there, but I couldn't guide myself by them. I'm certain of this from knowing and living with people who do live in their feelings. I see the richness and nuances of their experiences. Mine are very crude, but I'll match any of them for thinking.

Carl Jung, in his analysis of the structure of the psyche, has distinguished four psychological functions that link us to the outer world. These are sensation, thinking, feeling, and intuition. Sensation, he states, is the function that tells us that something exists; thinking, the function that tells us what it is; feeling, the function that evaluates its worth to us; and intuition, the function that enables us to estimate the possibilities inherent in the object or its situation.[71] Feeling, thus, is the inward guide to value; but its judgments are related normally to outward, empirical circumstance.[72]

The wonderful thing about symbology is that it includes all four functions. Jung speaks of a fifth, in the center, that he calls "the transcendent function." That's the one that symbols help you to attack. The symbol carries the thought to domains not of the head, but the head can lead it. I've been afraid that the other functions would interrupt the flow of this shell. It's a damn good craft I've got, but it can't do those other things.

I haven't meditated, and I know I have been afraid that meditation might open up lots of things that could delay the passage of this craft I'm rowing. It is an intentional limitation in order to go in a direction and get there. And I have gotten there, and I know it. Psychic experiences don't necessarily yield this kind of dimension. Each of us has individual capacities. The real trick is knowing the machinery of the boat in which you are crossing the channel.

The only way you can talk about this great tide in which you're a participant is as Schopenhauer did: the universe is a dream dreamed by a single dreamer where all the dream characters dream too.

WHEN we talk about scientific truth—just as when we talk about God—we are in trouble, because truth has different meanings. William James said, and it's valid , "Truth is what works."

The idea of Truth with a capital "T"—that there is something called Truth that's beyond the range of the relativity of the human mind trying to think—is what I call "the error of the found truth." The trouble with all of these damned preachers is the error of the found truth. When they get that tremolo in the voice and tell you what God has said, you know you've got a faker. When people think that they, or their guru, have The Truth—"This is It!"—they are what Nietzsche calls "epileptics of the concept": people who have gotten an idea that's driven them crazy.

Thinking you've got The Truth is a form of madness, as are pronouncements about absolute beauty, because one can easily see that there is no such thing. Beauty is always relevant to something. That quote from Keats' *Ode on a Grecian Urn*—"'Beauty is truth, truth beauty'—that is all ye know on earth, and all ye need to know."—it is a nice poetic thought, but what does it mean? Speaking of platitudes, I like Robert Bly's extrapolation of Descartes: "I think, therefore I am. The stone doesn't think, therefore it isn't."

Ideals are dangerous.

> Don't take them seriously.
> You can get by on a few.

A human being in action cannot represent perfection. You always represent one side of a duality that is itself perfection. The moment you take action, you are imperfect: you have decided to act that way instead of that other way. That's why people who think they are perfect are so ridiculous. They're in a bad position with respect to themselves.

It is a basic thought in India—it also turns up in China—that life itself is a sin, in this sense of its being imperfect. To live, you're killing and eating something, aren't you? You can reduce what you eat to fallen leaves if you want, but you're still eating life. You are taking the common good, you might say, and focusing it in your direction. And that is a decision on one side rather than on the other. So, decide to be imperfect, reconcile yourself to that, and go ahead. That's "joyful participation in the sorrows of the world."

The idea in India is that after many incarnations you achieve perfection and don't get reincarnated. You quit. You're out. Hence, all Buddhas are depicted more or less alike, because they all are perfect and don't reincarnate. As long as you're reincarnating, you are imperfect. So, you have to be loyal to your imperfection: find out what it is, then continue on your track. By being loyal to your part of the duality, you are keeping the mystery of history informed.

> Do not give up your vices.
> Make your vices work for you.
>
> If you are a proud person,
> don't get rid of your pride.
> Apply it to your spiritual quest.

The sublime in contrast to beauty? That which is beautiful does not threaten you. Even the terror of tragedy is not as threatening as something that blows you to pieces. The sublime is rendered by prodigious power or by enormous space: when you reach a mountaintop, for instance, and the world breaks open: a motif that is used in Buddhist art a great deal., and the reason temples are put on the top of hills. In Kyoto, there are gardens where you are screened from the expanding view while climbing, and suddenly—bing!— the whole vista opens before you. That's sublimity. So, power and space are two renditions of sublimity, and in both cases, the ego is diminished. It's strange: the less there is of you, the more you experience the sublime.

Coomaraswamy has a definition of art—"art is the making of things well"—that underlies art no matter what its function or category. If you're not interested in making things well, then you're not, even in the most elementary sense, an artist. I think Japanese machinery sells so well because the Japanese have that artistic idea. They strive for perfection and precision in everything.

The aim of art is perfection in the object. The Taj Mahal, for instance, is a grand artistic achievement. It's perfect. That's all there is to say about it. I had the advantage of seeing it first on a full-moon night, and I can't forget that moment. The damned thing is, I stood there and thought, "This is what Robinson Jeffers calls 'divinely superfluous beauty.' It's of no practical value in my life, but this moment is something in itself.

...the act of drinking tea is a normal, secular, common day affair; so also is sitting in a room with friends. And yet, consider what happens when you resolve to pay full attention to every single aspect of the act of drinking tea while sitting in

*a room with friends, selecting first your best, most appropriate
bowls, setting these down in the prettiest way, using an interesting pot, sharing with a few friends who go well together,
and providing things for them to look at: a few flowers perfectly composed, so that each will shine with its own beauty
and the organization of the group also will be radiant: a picture in accord, selected for the occasion: and perhaps an amusing little box, to open, shut, and examine from all sides.
Then, in preparing, serving, and drinking, every phase of the
action is rendered in such a gracefully functional manner that
all present may take joy in it, the common affair might well
be said to have been elevated to the status of a poem. And, in
fact, in the writing of a sonnet, words are used that are quite
normal, secular, common day tools. Just as in poetry, so in
tea: certain rules and manners have been developed as a consequence of ages of experience; and through a mastery of these,
immensely heightened powers of expression are achieved. For
as art imitates nature in its manner of operation, so does tea.*[73]*

*The guest approaches by the garden path, and must stoop
through the low entrance. He makes obeisance to the picture
or flower-arrangement, to the singing kettle, and takes his
place on the floor. The simplest object, framed by the controlled simplicity of the teahouse, stands out in mysterious
beauty, its silence holding the secret of temporal existence.
Each guest is permitted to complete the experience in relation
to himself. The members of the company thus contemplate the
universe in miniature, and become aware of their hidden
fellowship with immortals.*

*The great tea masters were concerned to make of the di-
vine wonder an experienced moment; then out of the teahouse
the influence was carried into the home; and out of the home
instilled into the nation.*[74]

In the fourth and fifth centuries B.C., "excellence in everything" was the Greek ideal. The gods represented excellencies in various categories. The golden mean was the middle way, "nothing in excess." I think excellence in living is a fine purpose. The Greeks were humanists. The Platonic mandate was "Know Thyself." The philosophical papers of that period have to do with conduct and virtue: virtue in the sense of excellence, not in the sense of good-versus-evil.

This is a point that Nietzsche brings out in *Beyond Good and Evil*. He distinguishes between what he calls "slave morality"—obeying a rule, doing what you're told, being good and not bad—and "master morality," which is equivalent to the Greek idea of virtue, and the Renaissance idea of *virtu*, and has to do with the kind of excellence achieved by one who is competent in something. I can remember somebody saying, "He's a good man." And somebody else asking, "Good for what?" That's a very important shift in accent. There is something exhilarating about the idea of sheer excellence and aggressive performance: "I get in there and do it!" in contrast to "Everything's okay, and I submit."

So, following Nietzsche, the lion of virtue is the one that tears a lamb to pieces, and the bad lion is the one that won't. But from the lamb's point of view, the bad lion is the one that eats him. And so, what you find in slave morality is that the people of excellence—the masterly ones—are regarded as bad. It really is so.

With the idea of the masterly ones, we get the idea of elitism. "Elitism? Elitism is bad." Have you ever heard that said? It's slave morality speaking. I recall lecturing at the University of Oklahoma to a select group of outstanding students from colleges all over the country. I'd never before had such an assemblage of excellent students. One of the professors later told me that one student came to him and said, "Having only excellent students in this group is elitism." The professor replied, "This program is for people who are up to the scholarship." "No," the student argued, "it's elitism and shouldn't be on this campus." So the professor said, "I'll tell you what I'll do, Bill. I'm going to recommend to the football coach that you play defensive halfback. What do you think?" He got the idea. The only place where excellence is appreciated is on the athletic field.

Around the eighteenth century, linguists discovered that almost all of the languages from India to Ireland, across that whole range, were of the Indo-European language family. At the time, they did not know how ancient civilization is—the Mesopotamian region and Egyptian civilization had not yet been explored—but it was evident that the Greek, Roman, and European civilizations were all out of the impulse of the Indo-European peoples. And so, a Frenchman came up with the idea of a master race. The idea of Aryan supremacy that Hitler later picked up had to do with this idea of a master race. It had nothing to do with master morality or slave morality. But Hitler used Nietszche's words, which is very unfortunate, because Nietzsche absolutely despised anti-Semitism and the idea of the state. In fact, he said, "The new idol is the state." And that's what Hitler represented. A horrible little man. His ideas were not Nietzsche's.

PSYCHOLOGY is a means of interpretation, a way of interpreting what's going on. Are you going to interpret it as the work of a concrete deity up there who has brought it about? Is that concrete deity a fact? How did it get there? That diety has to be interpreted psychologically, so that you know that what we'e talking about is not "out there," but "in here."

It was for me a startling experience, as it must have been for many others watching at that time the television broadcast of the Apollo space-flight immediately before that of Armstrong's landing on the moon, when Ground Control in Houston asked, "Who's navigating now?" and the answer that came back was, "Newton!"

I was reminded of Immanuel Kant's discussion of space in his Prolegomena to Any Future Metaphysic, *where he asks: "How is it that in this space, here, we can make judgments that we know with apodictic certainty will be valid in that space, there?"[75]*

Kant's reply to the question was that the laws of space are known to the mind because they are of the mind. They are of a knowledge that is within us from birth, a knowledge a priori, which is only brought to recollection by apparently external circumstance....

In other words, it then occurred to me that outer space is within us inasmuch as the laws of space are within us; outer and inner space are the same. We know, furthermore, that we have actually been born from space, since it was out of primordial space that the galaxy took form, of which our life-giving sun is a member. And this earth, of whose material we are made, is a flying satellite of that sun. We are, in fact, productions of this earth. We are, as it were, its organs. Our eyes are the eyes of this earth; our knowledge is the earth's knowledge. And the earth, as we now know, is a production of space....

And so now we must ask: What does all this do to mythology? Obviously, some corrections have to be made.

For example: It is believed that Jesus, having risen from the dead, ascended physically to heaven (Luke 24:51), to be followed shortly by his mother in her sleep (Early Christian belief, confirmed as Roman Catholic dogma on November 1, 1950). It is also written that some nine centuries earlier, Elijah, riding a chariot of fire, had been carried to heaven in a whirlwind (2 Kings 2:11).

Now, even ascending at the speed of light, which for a physical body is impossible, those three celestial voyagers would not yet be out of the galaxy. Dante in the year A.D. 1300 spent the Easter weekend in a visit to hell, purgatory, and heaven; but that voyage was in spirit alone, his body remaining on earth. Whereas Jesus, Mary, and Elijah are declared to have ascended physically. What is to be made today of such mythological (hence, metaphorical) folk ideas?

Obviously, if anything of value is to be made of them at all (and I submit that the elementary original idea must have been something of this kind), where those bodies went was not into outer space, but into inner space. That is to say, what is connoted by such metaphorical voyages is the possibility of a return of the mind in spirit, while still incarnate, to full knowledge of that transcendent source out of which the mystery of a given life arises into this field of time and back into which it in time dissolves. It is an old, old story in mythology: of the Alpha and Omega that is the ground of all being, to be realized as the beginning and end of this life.[76]

The limits of psychology are the same as the limits of theology. They have to do with the problem of symbolization, not with the transcendence, and they go the same distance. When you simply translate God into a psychological function or factor, you have gone as far as God and no further. As long as you have a God, you're stuck. Recall Meister Eckhart: "The ultimate leave-taking is the leaving of God for God."

It's a shame we have only one word for the two concepts. In India, there are several—jiva, Atman, Brahman—and they are all different. "God," our one word, is a really inadequate word. It always implies a personification, and unless one says "Goddess," it implies a male personification. Our limited vocabulary is what binds us, what ties us up.

In relation to the first books and chapters of the Bible, it used to be the custom of both Jews and Christians to take the narratives literally, as though they were dependable accounts of the origin of the universe and of actual prehistoric events. It was supposed and taught that there had been, quite concretely, a creation of the world in seven days by a god known only to the Jews; that somewhere on this broad new earth there had been a Garden of Eden containing a serpent that could talk; that the first woman, Eve, was formed from the first man's rib, and that the wicked serpent told her of the marvelous properties of the fruits of a certain tree of which God had forbidden the couple to eat; and that, as a consequence of their having eaten of that fruit, there followed a "Fall" of all mankind, death came into the world, and the couple was driven forth from the garden. For there was in the center of that garden a second tree, the fruit of which would have given them eternal life; and their creator, fearing lest they should now take and eat of that too, and so become as knowing and immortal as himself, cursed them, and having driven them out, placed at his garden gate "cherubim and a flaming sword which turned every way to guard the way to the tree of life."[77]

Those cherubim are an important symbol. The Garden of innocence and spontaneous life, of unity before the knowledge of pairs of opposites, exits into the world of time and historical duality, symbolized by the cherubim at the gate with the flaming sword between: you can't go through. How are we to interpret those cherubim and the Garden?

Well, you go to Japan to see the Great Buddha at Nara He is seated in the garden at the foot of the Tree of Immortal Life. As you approach the temple, you come to a preliminary building where two terrific figures stand as door guardians. They are the cherubim. One of them has his mouth open, the other's mouth is closed: a pair of opposites. One represents the fear of death, and the other the desire for life—the temptations that didn't touch the Buddha.

No earthly paradise has been found....for it is the garden of man's soul. As pictured in the Bible tale with its four mysterious rivers flowing in the four directions from a common source at the center, it is exactly what C. G. Jung has called an "archetypal image": a psychological symbol, spontaneously produced, which appears universally, both in dreams and in myths and rites....Like the image of a deity, the quadrated garden with the life source at its center is a figment of the psyche, not a product of gross elements, and the one who seeks without for it, gets lost.[78]

So what is keeping you out of the Garden? Your fear and desire: that which the Buddha transcended. And when the Buddha did not respond to temptations of fear and desire, he passed through the gate to the tree, where he now sits with his hand pointing to the earth. That's redemption. The Buddha and the Christ are equivalent. Jesus has gone through and become, himself, the fruit of the tree.

> When threatened
> by fear and desire,
> let ego go.

So the idea of redemption in both Christianity and Buddhism has to do with one's having come through. Whether one does or not, in either tradition, is something else. You can walk between those figures at Nara and enter the temple, bringing fear and desire with you, and you've not really gone through. You may think you've achieved illumination, but you're still in exile.

The Buddhist interpretation of this whole thing is one of psychological transformation. The Christian interpretation is one of debt and payment. Paul was preaching to a group of merchants, who understood the whole mystery in terms of economics: there is a debt, and you get an equivalent payment. The debt is enormous, so the payment has to be enormous This is all bankers' thinking. Christianity is caught up in that.

I see Buddhism and Christianity as two vocabularies for speaking about the same thing. In Buddhism we are lost in the world of fear and desire, the field of maya, illusion. This is, in Christian iconography, the Fall. Redemption is losing those fears and having the experience of eternal life. You experience that through the act of Jesus in affirming the world, in participating in the world with joy.

The Buddha is saying, "Don't be afraid of those gate guardians. Come in and eat the fruit of the tree." The act of communion is eating the fruit of the second tree in the Garden. The fruit is symbolic of the spiritual nourishment that comes when you have reached the knowledge of your eternal life. There are various ways of interpreting these mysteries. I am not telling you something I invented.

"Since in the world of time every man lives but one life, it is in himself that he must search for the secret of the Garden."—Loren Eisely[79]

...in the Levant, the accent is on obedience, the obedience of man to the will of God, whimsical though it might be; the leading idea being that the god has rendered a revelation, which is registered in a book that men are to read and to revere, never to presume to criticize, but to accept and to obey.

Those who do not know, or who would reject, this holy book are in exile from their maker. [80]

So, then, what is it that our religions actually teach? Not the way to an experience of identity with the Godhead, since that, as we have said, is the prime heresy; but the way and the means to establish and maintain a relationship to a named God. And how is such a relationship to be achieved? Only through membership in a certain supernaturally endowed, uniquely favored social group. [81]

A religion of relationships
is a religion of exile.

The Old Testament God has a covenant with a certain historic people, the only holy race—the only holy thing, in fact—on earth. And how does one gain membership? The traditional answer was most recently (March 10, 1970) reaffirmed in Israel as defining the first prerequisite to full citizenship in that mythologically inspired nation: by being born of a Jewish mother. [82]

Our actual ultimate root [83]
is in our humanity,
not in our personal genealogy.

And in the Christian view, by what means? By virtue of the incarnation of Christ Jesus, who is to be known as true God and true man (which, in the Christian view, is a miracle, whereas in the Orient, on the other hand, everyone is to be known as true God and true man, though few may have yet awakened to the force of that wonder in themselves). [84]

We are all Christs
and don't realize it.

Among tribesmen depending on the hunting skills of individuals for their existence, the individual is fostered: even the concept of immortality is individual, not collective. Spiritual leadership is exercised primarily by shamans, who are individuals endowed with spiritual power through personal experience, not socially installed priests, made members of an organization through appointment and anointment.[85]

The central demand is to surrender our exclusivity: everything that defines us as against each other. For years people have used religious affiliations to do this. Martin Buber speaks of "I-Thou" and "I-It" relationships. An ego talking to a *Thou* is different from an ego talking to an *It*. Wherever we emphasize otherness or outgroups, we are making persons into *Its*: the gentile, the Jew, the enemy—they all become the same.

Totem, tribal, racial, and aggressively missionizing cults represent only partial solutions of the psychological problem of subduing hate by love: they only partially initiate. Ego is not annihilated in them; rather, it is enlarged; instead of thinking only of himself, the individual becomes dedicated to the whole of his society. The rest of the world meanwhile (that is to say, by far the greater portion of mankind) is left outside the sphere of his sympathy and protection because outside the sphere of the protection of his god. And there takes place, then, that dramatic divorce of the two principles of love and hate which the pages of history so bountifully illustrate. Instead of clearing his own heart the zealot tries to clear the world.[86]

> If you fix
> on yourself and your tradition,
> believing you alone have got "It,"
> you've removed yourself
> from the rest of mankind.

Some say Communism is a social system without a religion; but you can't say that Communism is not religious, for the laws of a Communist society have all the qualities of a religion because Communism has become the religion.

In terms of the ritual side of it, Communism has all the character of a religion, and it has the characteristics of one that is a biblical descendent. There is a good and there is a bad, and we're fighting for the good, and there will be a day, come the Revolution, when all will be Communist and right. Part of the argument between Russia and China is about who is interpreting Marx properly, which is sheer scholasticism.

So, actually, most of the world's societies are being ruled by post-biblical traditions, in which anybody who is anything else is out. Besides the Communist brotherhood, there is the Jewish community, the Christian community, and the Islamic, the Muslim community. Judaism doesn't have a missionizing impulse, but the other three—Islam, Christianity, and Communism— are murderous traditions. The aim of each is total world conquest. That's a beautiful show. Makes a mess of the world though.

> The goal of life
> is to make your heartbeat
> match the beat of the universe,
> to match your nature with Nature.

In Buddhism the goal of life is the repose of the nir-*vanic* experience of life: "joyful participation in the sorrows of the world," and soon. In a credo religion, the goal of life tends to get formulated. In Islam, it's in the very name of the religion: *Islām* means "submission," to bow in acquiescence and reverence to the will of God. This credo gives warriors enormous courage and power: whether they're going to get killed or not get killed, they move in with submission to the fate. In fact, that's what a warrior has to do anyhow.

> The warrior's approach
> is to say "yes" to life:
> "yea" to it all.

In terms of historical action, Christianity and Islam have the same character. They're going to remake the world for their God. I find this repulsive, but it's what makes history, so you have to say "yes" to it. If you say "no" to one little detail of your life, you've unraveled the whole thing. You have to say "yes" to the whole thing, including its extinction. That's what's known as "joyful participation in the sorrows of the world." It's my little theme song.

> Love informs the whole universe
> right down into the abyss of hell.

*D*ante in his Divine Comedy *unfolded a vision of the universe that perfectly satisfied both the approved religious and the accepted scientific notions of his time. When Satan had been flung out of heaven for his pride and disobedience, he was supposed to have fallen like a flaming comet and, when he struck the earth, to have plowed right through to its center. The prodigious crater that he opened thereupon became the fiery pit of Hell; and the great mass of displaced earth pushed forth at the opposite pole became the Mountain of Purgatory, which is represented by Dante as lifting heavenward exactly at the South Pole.*[87]

Dante saw even the fires of hell
as a manifestation of God's love.

You will have heard the old legend of how, when God created the angels, he commanded them to pay worship to no one but himself; but then, creating man, he commanded them to bow in reverence to this most noble of his works, and Lucifer refused—because, we are told, of his pride. However, according to the Moslem reading of his case, it was rather because he loved and adored God so deeply and intensely that he could not bring himself to bow before anything else. And it was for that that he was flung into Hell, condemned to exist there forever, apart form his love.[88]

Satan is the epitome of infractible ego.

The Persian poets have asked, "By what power is Satan sustained?" And the answer that they have found is this: "By his memory of the sound of God's voice when he said, 'Be gone!'" What an image of that exquisite spiritual agony which is at once the rapture and the anguish of love![89]

"*The God that holds you over the Pit of Hell, much as one holds a spider or some lothsome Insect over the Fire, abhors you, and is dreadfully provoked; his Wrath towards you burns like Fire; he looks upon you as Worthy of nothing else but to be cast into the Fire; he is of purer Eyes than to bear to have you in his Sight; you are Ten Thousand Times so abominable in his Eyes as the most hateful venomous Serpent is in ours....you are thus in the Hands of an angry god; 'tis nothing but his mere Pleasure that keeps you from being at this Moment swallowed up in everlasting Destruction.*" — Pastor Jonathan Edwards[90]*

"God's mere pleasure," which defends the sinner from the arrow, the flood, and the flames, is termed in the traditional vocabulary of Christianity God's "mercy"; and "the mighty power of the spirit of God," by which the heart is changed, that is God's "grace." In most mythologies, the images of mercy and grace are rendered as vividly as those of justice and wrath, so that a balance is maintained, and the heart is buoyed rather than scourged along its way. "Fear not!" says the hand gesture of the god Shiva, as he dances before his devotee the dance of the universal destruction. "Fear not, for all rests well in God. The forms that come and go—and of which your body is but one—are the flashes of my dancing limbs. Know Me in all, and of what shall you be afraid?"[91]

Hell is the concretization of your life experiences, a place where you're stuck, the wasteland. In hell, you are so bound to yourself that grace cannot enter.

> The problem with hell
> is that the fire doesn't consume you.
> The fires of transformation do.

Fire is symbolic of the night sea journey, the up-coming of shadow—repressed biography, history, and traumas—and the burning out of the imps of malice. Purgatory is a place where that fire is turned into a purging fire that burns out the fear system, burns out the blockage so that it will open.

If hell is the wasteland, then purgatory would be the journey where you leave the place of pain. You are still in pain, but you're in quest with a sense of possible realization. There is no longer despair. You really do not have a sacred place, a rescue land, until you can find some little field of action, or place to be, where it's not a wasteland, where there is a little spring of ambrosia. It's a joy that comes from inside. It is not something that puts the joy in you, but a place that lets you so experience your own will, your own intention, and your own wish that, in small, the joy is there. The sin against the Holy Ghost, I think, is despair. The Holy Ghost is that which inspires you to realization., and despair is the feeling that nothing can come. That is absolute hell.

Find a place where there's joy,
and the joy will burn out the pain.

I had an interesting experience when I was lecturing at the Foreign Service Institute in Washington D.C. to groups of officers about to go on assignment to the Orient or Southeast Asia. In one group there was this very smart black man, who'd just come from three years in Vienna and was going to India. The gentlemen in these groups would always invite me to have lunch at a very nice restaurant at the Watergate Hotel, and this time they asked this chap to drive me over there.

He had a zoom-zoom sports car, and he was quite the guy. When he and I were at the table, the first thing he started talking to me about was being black and the things that were against him. I thought, "Well, I'm going to let him have it. I'm sick of this kind of stuff." I said, "In terms of the people I know, you are way up there. You've got a good life. Everybody has something against him. Some people are unattractive, and that's against them. Some people are Protestants in a Catholic country; some are Catholic in a Protestant environment. If you go on blaming everything that is negative in your life on the fact that you're black, you deny yourself the privilege of becoming human. You're just a black man. You are not a man yet." Then the crowd came in, and he sat quietly the rest of the time.

When I arrived the next month for my session, I went up to report in, and the officer on duty said, "Say, Joe, what did you tell that guy last time?" I said, "Oh, I don't know. Why?" He said, "Well, he's bought all your books, and he's downstairs and wants you to sign them. When I asked him why he was doing that, he said, 'Professor Campbell has made a man out of me.'"

Now that was a big lesson to me, and it runs against all this bleeding-heart stuff. I was proud of that. So, he'd been stuck in his hell: he hadn't been able to see past his own notion of what his limitation was. Anyway, I went downstairs, and he had all the books, and as I was signing them, I said, "Well, this'll help you remember me." He said, "Oh, I'll never forget you."

Everytime you do something like that you find it was the right thing to do, provided that you furnish the person with something to jump to. If you're really not interested in the person, you can just agree with them, "Ah, you poor chap, I understand. It's real tough."

> Don't think of what's being said,
> but of what's talking.
> Malice? Ignorance? Pride? Love?
>
> The goal of the hero's journey
> is yourself, finding yourself.

When we are one place in our lives and want to be in another place, there's an obstacle to be overcome, a threshold to be passed. The six-pointed star, which in Judaism is the Star of David, is a symbol that appears in India as the sign of Chakra IV.

In the double triangle, the upward-pointed triangle —you might use the word "aspiration" for that—is symbolic of the movement principle. The downward-pointed triangle is inertia, and it represents what the obstacle would be. The downward-pointing triangle can be experienced either as an impediment or as the door that is opened. When you recognize its psychological significance and effect a mental transformation, then you see the obstacle as an opening.

So you can experience the downward-pointed triangle two ways: one, as an obstacle; and the other, as the means by which you are going to make the ascent. So, everything in your life that seems to be obstructive can be transformed by your recognizing that it is the means for your transition.

That's the whole sense of the Tantra philosophy in India. Tantric exercises, which are occult and hidden, go so far as to propose precisely the most destructive, or seductive practices, as the rung of a ladder of ascent. So, for example, sexual union, which is usually one of the chief distractions from the way, is taken to be the way. Also you have—and this is extreme—necrophagia, the eating of dead bodies.

In certain American Indian cultures of the Southwest, one of the initiations to the clown category—and their black and white costume motif is a good symbol of the clown—involves actually eating dog shit. The most repulsive has to be accepted as also Brahman. People like that are beyond all pairs of opposites. You can go to quite an extreme in eliminating your resistance to some of the things that life proposes. But you don't have to go that far.

In the Gnostic *Gospel According to Thomas*, Jesus says, "Cleave a piece of wood, I am there; lift up the stone and you will find me there."[92] The historical Jesus has identified himself with the Christ. That is Buddha consciousness. He is living in terms, not of his ego, but of the Christ: the ubiquity in everything of the radiance of that which is the deepest center within you.

So, when this downward-pointed triangle becomes the means, instead of the obstruction, to your breakthrough, you've achieved the passage of the threshold.

> There is always danger
> at the threshold.
> Leave the temporal body,
> and let the spirit enter.

What is the obstruction in your life, and how do you transform it into the radiance? Ask yourself, "What is the main obstruction to my path?" In India, demons are really obstructions to the expansion of consciousness. A demon or devil is a power in you to which you have not given expression, an unrecognized or suppressed god. Anyone who is unable to understand a god sees it as a devil.

> "Devil" is a word we use
> for another peoples' god.

All anyone is really trying to do is have an expansion of consciousness, so that the knowing and loving are on greater and greater horizons. That's what happens when the Kundalini comes up: more and more of the body is informed with radiance and consciousness.

> The goal of the journey
> is to discover yourself
> as consciousness.

Joyce says in *Ulysses*, "If you can put your five fingers through it, it is a gate, if not a door."[93]   The difficulties one encounters may be looked at as having the possibility of transformation into opening gates rather than closed doors.

When you find yourself blocked by a concretized symbol from your childhood, meditation is a systematic discipline that will solve your problem. The function of meditation, ideally, would be to transcend the concretized response and deliver the message.

The first thing I'd do would be to think, "What are, specifically, the symbols that are still active, still touching me this way?" What are the symbols? There's a great context of symbols in the world. Not all of them are the ones that afflict you. When you do find the symbol that is blocking you, find some mode of thinking and experience that matches in its importance for you what the symbol meant. You cannot get rid of a symbol if you haven't found that to which it refers.

If you find in your own heart a center of experience for which the symbol has been substituted, the symbol will dissolve. Think, "Of what is it the metaphor?" When you find that, the symbol will lose its blocking force, or it will become a guide.

This is the "knowing" part of "to know, to love, to serve." If you're in trouble with this part because you do not really know what this thing refers to, then it will push you around. I'm very, very sure of that.

To dissolve such a concretization as an adult, you need to find what the reference of the symbol is. When that is found, you will have the elucidation. The symbol will move into place, and you can regard it with pleasure: as something that guides you to the realization of what its message is, instead of as a roadblock. This is an important point.

That is the downward-pointed triangle. It is either an obstruction or the field through which the realization is to come.

Heaven and hell are psychological definitions. The Catholic definition of mortal sin should relieve you of the thought that you have committed one. As a Catholic, you learn that for a sin to be mortal, the kind that condemns you to hell, it has to be a grievous matter, over which there has been sufficient reflection, done with full consent of the will. So, a mortal sin is a deliberate exclusion of the gift of grace, and that is what the devil symbolizes. You cannot open to supernatural grace, to the voice of God.

Deliberately breaking the ritual law can be a mortal sin. But here's the bizarre thing about such a religion of ritual laws: kill your mother in a passion, and that is not a mortal sin. That's a venial sin, and you will have your two-thousand years in purgatory on that one. But one little mortal sin, and you're bound for hell. Let's all go in a big chariot. When the Church said that eating meat on Friday was no longer a mortal sin, there was a crisis in the entire Catholic community. In New York City, where there are a lot of Catholics, there was a great crisis, part of which had to do with the fish merchants.

> When the symbols are interpreted
> spiritually rather than concretely,
> then they yield the revelation.

I want to tell about my relationship to confession. As a kid, you go to confession, and you say, "Bless me, Father, for I have sinned. I disobeyed Mother three times, didn't say morning prayers two mornings, and told a lie." He says, "You mustn't do these things. Say five Our Fathers and five Hail Marys, and you're clear."

I never got old enough to confess any significant sin. I don't know what the hell would have happened. I did commit one little sin one summer, at Shelter Island out on Long Island. I was about nine years old. There was a wonderful hardware store named Ferguson's. I remember it well. I'd go there with my mother and see her buy things. She'd say, "Charge it," and then go out with them. One such trip, I saw a wonderful penknife with all these things on it. So a few days later I went in alone and said, "I want that knife." the owner said, "Here, Joe." I said, "Charge it." He said, "Okay."

I went home and said to Mother, "Look at the wonderful penknife I found." She said, "Are you sure you found that?" I said, "Yes, yes, I found it." Well, at the end of the month a bill came for the penknife, and Mother said, "Joe, come here. When you go to confession on Saturday, take that penknife to Father Isadore, confess the sin, and then take the knife around to the sacristy and give it to him."

This was not easy. It was the most severe indication of what I'd done. Five Our Fathers and five Hail Marys were nothing like giving up that knife. So, I went to confession and tried to tell the priest what I had done. I was an altar boy at the time: you know, "mea culpa, mea culpa" stuff. Afterward, I went around to the sacristy and gave him the penknife. And he said, "Oh, Joe, I didn't know it was that serious."

I knew something then that I didn't know before I stole that penknife: charging it without any idea of what the hell was going to happen was wonderful.

The forgiveness in Roman Catholic confession is conditional. The absolution the priest gives is conditional on a resolution on your part.

First, you need contrition, meaning you are really, really sorry for having committed that sin. Second, you make a resolution never to commit it again. That does not mean that you are not going to commit it again. It means that you sincerely resolve not to.

In that wonderful Arthurian Romance of *La Questa del St. Graal*, where all the knights go out to discover the Grail, Lancelot could not behold the Grail. Why? Because of his adulterous affair with Guinevere. But the real reason was that he could not honestly feel contrition for that love. How could Lancelot possibly have contrition for having experienced through Guinevere an illumination beyond what even the church had given him? And it is represented as such. He could not feel sorry, and he could not resolve to cancel it, so he was unworthy to behold the Grail.

> The Grail is being in perfect accord
> with the abundance of nature,
> the highest spiritual realization,
> the inexhaustible vessel from which
> you get everything you want.
>
> In a religion of duality,
> the sin and eternal punishment
> comes from the outside,
> from the ruling concrete god.

There's a knight in mortal sin. And yet, the monk who wrote that Romance had a sense of the charm of Lancelot's life: he's the most human, the most touching

161

character in the whole context. These are ironical things, which is why, finally, the priest says, "God's will? We don't know God's will. There may be forgiveness that we don't know anything about."

> I will hold this love against God,
> eternal damnation, anything.
> That is true love.

When I was about sixteen years old, in prep school, and knew I was losing my childhood faith, I resolved that I would not quit the Catholic church until I knew why I was quitting, that is to say, until I had dissolved the symbols and knew what they referred to and meant. The whole thing wasn't over until I was twenty-five years old and in Germany. I spent nine years working everything out, and then it just dropped off like a worn-out shirt. That's the knowing thing. If you don't know what the hell that symbol is saying to you, then it's just there as a command, and there is going to be more and more of this hanging on. If you can't use your mind in this rather complex field, I don't know how you are going to work it out.

> You become mature
> when you become
> the authority for your own life.

COULD God exist if nobody else did? No. That's why gods are very avid for worshipers. If there is nobody to worship them, there are no gods. There are as many gods as there are people thinking about God. When Mrs. Mulligan and the Pope are thinking about God, it is not the same God.

> In choosing your god, you choose
> your way of looking at the universe.
> There are plenty of Gods.
> Choose yours.

> The god you worship
> is the god you deserve.

When you say that God needs man and man needs God, that "God" that's being talked about is the image of God, the concept of God, the name of God, the ethnic God. You bet he needs man. He wouldn't be there if it weren't for man.

> In the tribe, deities were
> personifications of power.
> In later years,
> they became the source of power.

> All the gods of the world are
> metaphors, not powers.

All imaging of God, if the word is going to mean anything besides "this is what Mother taught me," is supposed to refer to that which transcends all knowledge, all naming, all forming; and, consequently, the word has to point past itself. In our tradition, the idea of God is so strongly personified as a person that you get stuck with that problem whenever you think of God.

> God is not an illusion,
> but a symbol pointing beyond itself
> to the realization of the mystery
> of at-one-ment.

Jung, in his book *Answer to Job*, deals with the image of God that has come down through the centuries. How can we relate to it? Well, the Old Testament image, Yahweh, is of a lawgiver, a very strong dictator, an angry father. And in the Book of Job, you have the epitomization of that image.

Here is this Job, who has been a good man, and Yahweh, the God, boasting to the devil, Satan, says: "Have you considered Job? How loyal he is to me? How he loves me?" And Satan says, "Well, you've been pretty good to him. Make it tough and see how long this is going to last." Yawheh says, "I bet ya." And Satan says, "I bet ya."

Gilbert Murray has commented: "It's as though someone says, 'My dog won't bite me no matter what I do.' And someone else says, 'I bet he will.' The dog's master says, 'I bet he won't.' And the other person says, 'Get going now, see how badly you can abuse him, and then see if he won't bite you.'"

So that's the situation, and after the wager, things get rough. What a time Job has! His family is killed, his wealth is taken from him, and he ends up on a heap of ashes with a case of boils. His friends, his so-called "comforters," annoy him further by saying, "You must have been a pretty bad chap to deserve all this." He says, "No, I'm good." And he's right: he *is* good.

Well, with this challenge to God, he finally has to come through and show himself. I mean, it's a big deal. So, God shows himself, and what does he say? He says, "Who are you, you little worm, to question me? How dare you even consider that you could understand what is happening to you? Could you fill Leviathan's nose with harpoons? I did it. Try it."

Job is completely cowed. He suspends human judgment. He says, "I have heard of you with the hearing of my ears. Now I behold you with my eyes, and I am ashamed. I cover my head with ashes."

Now, reading that in terms of its real spiritual message, what it means is that you cannot judge your destiny in terms of something that was done to you by somebody. I mean, what is actually happening there— although it is not admitted—is that the image of God as a person is exploded. When you get to the transpersonal, you can't speak of "justice" and "injustice."

What about all the landslides along the Big Sur coastline and the millions of dollars of damage they've caused? If you take these acts of nature as something that somebody has done to the people living there, you have the whole thing messed up. But that's not the way the *Book of Job* has been understood. It has been understood in the way of submission to a *person*. And a person who would pull a deal like that on somebody is a pretty unappetizing type.

Actually, the *Book of Job*, which dates from around the fifth century B.C., is anticipated by a Babylonian text from about 1500 B.C. called the "Babylonian Job," in which a king, who has been sacrificing to the deities and building them temples, has been overcome by, I think it was, leprosy. He tries to interpret his affliction in terms of what he has done in worship as a payment. Now, if you think of worship as a form of payment for something, you're on the wrong track altogether. The *Book of Job* really breaks down that idea. But if you are going to hold to the image of God that is presented in the *Book of Job*, you have something that needs a little bit of refinement.

So then the Christians, as a next step, take the idea of the Incarnation of the second person of the Blessed Trinity offering himself in love to the world to be a higher, more illuminated, form. In other words, God has been tempered by taking the form of man and experiencing the world of man.

But, says our friend Jung, this is not the answer either, because Christ was a divine incarnation born of a virgin, so he really wasn't man, he was God. Yet, Jung argues, "God wanted to become man and still wants to." So he provided for his continuing incarnation, as it were, within man as the Holy Ghost, the third person of the Blessed Trinity. So, if you want to see God in the world, recognize it in mankind. That's the essence of Jung's answer to Job: Don't throw this blame back on God, on the universe, or on anything of the kind. Realize that all notions of God are historically conditioned images for qualities that are to be recognized as actually being in man.

"The incarnation in Christ is the prototype which is continually being transferred to the creature by the Holy Ghost."—Jung[94]

There is a darling little woman who comes to my lectures in New York, who was a nun. She left the convent after hearing a couple of my talks. She did. That's one of my great credits, you old bastard up there. The last time I was lecturing and she was in the group, she came up to me afterward and asked, "Mr. Campbell, do you think that Jesus was God, was God's son?" I said, "Not unless we all are." "Ahh!" she said, and off she went.

And that's what Jung is saying in his *Answer to Job* : it is actually the work of man that is projected in the image of an imagined being called God. And so, historically, the God image is really a mirror image of the condition of man at a given time.

Yet, I think most people take their image of God very concretely. Except for the French. A survey was taken in which people were asked, "Do you believe in God? Do you believe in hell?" The French—I think, seventy-five percent of them—did not believe in God, but did believe in hell! I like Alan Watts' reply: "If you believe in God, I don't. If you don't, I do."

My belief is that nobody experiences the ultimate rapture, because it's beyond pairs of opposites, so if anyone did, there'd be nobody there anyhow. Jung is amusing on that point. "If you go beyond subject and object," he wonders, "who is there to have the experience?" I think to give oneself a ground for anything other than monastic living, all one has to do is realize that such a thing is implied; that is to say, a mystery that is beyond subject, object, and all pairs of opposites is the mystery on the ground of which we ride.

When the physicist explores the depths of the atom or the outer reaches of space, he discovers pairs of opposites and mysteries that science hasn't been able to penetrate. When it does penetrate to the next level, it's still mysterious. They've got so many sub-atomic particles. One is named after Joyce's "quark." It seems to me that's about as mysterious as you can get. There is the transcendent. Know it's there, and then don't worry about it. Simply behold the radiance everywhere.

People know there is a way to have this spiritual development take place, but the Church is not helping us do it, because it's talking about metaphorical events as if they were historical facts. The Pope is having a hard time now because nobody believes any of it. Who believes in the Virgin Birth? The Virgin Birth is metaphorical, and so is the Ascension. Sure, I can believe in the Ascension of Jesus, but I've turned the outer space into the inner space: he went into the place where heaven is: right inside. His Ascension represents the inward, mythological journey. And the Virgin Birth refers to the birth of the spiritual life in the human.

"...this birth befalls in the soul exactly as it does in eternity, neither more nor less, for it is the same birth: this birth befalls in the ground and essence of the soul.[95]
"God is in all things as being, as activity, as power. but he is procreative in the soul alone; for though every creature is a vestige of God, the soul is the natural image of God.... Such perfection as enters the soul, whether it be divine light, grace, or bliss, must needs enter the soul in this birth and no other wise. Do but foster this birth in thee and thou wilt experience all good and all comfort, all happiness, all being, and all truth. What comes to thee therein brings the true being and stability; and whatsoever thou mayest seek or grasp without it perishes, take it how thou wilt."—M. Eckhart[96]

That font of life is the core of the individual, and within himself he will find it—if he can tear the coverings away.[97]

The idea that we will have a divine visitation by some friendly forms, benign forces from other planets who will come to our aid and save us, is a clear reflection of an outmoded understanding of the universe.

Jung wrote that the modern myth of unidentified flying objects tells us something of humankind's visionary expectations. People are looking for visits from the outside world because they think our deliverance will come from there. But the space age reminds us that voyages into outer space turn us back to inner space. The Kingdom of God is within us, but we have this idea that the gods act from "out there."

> The Kingdom of the Father is not
> going to come through expectation.
>
> We bring it about in our own hearts.
>
> [98]The Kingdom is here.
>
> One looks at the world
> and sees the radiance.
>
> The Easter revelation is right there.
> We don't have to wait
> for something to happen.

What has always been basic to Easter, or resurrection, is crucifixion. If you want resurrection, you must have crucifixion. Too many interpretations of the Crucifixion have failed to emphasize that relationship and emphasize instead the calamity of the event. If you emphasize the calamity, you look for someone to blame, which is why people have blamed the Jews. But crucifixion is not a calamity if it leads to new life. Through Christ's crucifixion we were unshelled, which enabled us to be born to resurrection. That is not a calamity. So, we must take a fresh look at this event if its symbolism is to be sensed.

If we think of the Crucifixion only in historical terms, we lose the symbol's immediate reference to ourselves. Jesus left his mortal body on the cross, the sign of earth, to go to the Father, with whom he was one. We, similarly, are to identify with the eternal life within us. The symbol also tells us of God's willing acceptance of the cross, that is to say, of his participation in the trials and sorrows of human life in the world, so that he is here within us, not by way of a fall or mistake, but with rapture and joy. Thus the cross has dual sense: one, of our going to the divine; the other, of the coming of the divine to us. It is a true crossing.

In the Christian tradition, Christ's crucifixion is a major problem: Why could the savior not have just come? Why did he have to be crucified?

Well, various theological explanations have come down to us, but I think an adequate and proper one can be found in Paul's Epistle to the Philippians, where he writes in chapter 2 that Christ did not think that Godhood was something to be held to—which is to say, neither should you—but rather, yielding, he took the form of a servant even to death on the cross. This is joyful affirmation of the sufferings of the world. The imitation of Christ, then, is participating in the suffering and joys of the world, all the while seeing through them the radiance of the divine presence. That's operating from the heart chakra, where the two triangles are joined together.

That's what I see in the Crucifixion. Of all the explanations I've read, it is the only one that makes, what I would call, respectable sense. The others are all concerned with a wrathful god who has to be appeased by the sacrifice of his son. What do you do with a thing like that? It is a translation of the sacrifice into a very crude image. The idea of God being entity that has to be appeased is just too nasty a concretion.

Christ's crucifixion,
his going to the Father, the spirit,
is not something
that should not have happened.

It must happen.

The hero's death and resurrection
is a model for
the casting off of the old life
and moving into the new.

*Not the animal world, not the plant world, not the
miracle of the spheres, but man himself is now the crucial
mystery. Man is that alien presence with whom the forces of
egoism must come to terms, through whom the ego is to be
crucified and resurrected, and in whose image society is to be
reformed. Man, understood however not as "I" but as
"Thou": for the ideals and temporal institutions of no tribe,
race, continent, social class, or century, can be the measure of
the inexhaustible and multifariously wonderful divine
existence that is the life in all of us.*[99]

The central truth about Easter and Pass-
over, which have the same roots, is that we're all called
out of the house of bondage, even as the Jews were
called out of their bondage in Egypt. We are called out
of bondage to our old traditions in the way in which the
moon throws off its shadow to emerge anew, in the
way life throws off the shadow of death. Easter is not
Easter and Passover is not Passover, unless they release
us even from the tradition that gives us these feasts.

> Easter and Passover
> make us experience in ourselves
> a call out of bondage.
>
> So experiencing them
> doesn't destroy
> our religious traditions.
>
> Understanding these symbols
> in their transcendent spiritual sense
> enables us to see our traditions freshly
> and to possess them anew.

Easter and Passover are prime symbols of what we
are faced with in the space age. We're challenged both
mystically and socially, because our ideas of the universe have been reordered by our experience in space.
The consequence is that we can no longer hold onto the
religious symbols that we formulated when we thought
that the earth was the center of the universe.

> The misunderstanding is reading
> spiritual mythological symbols
> as though they were references
> to historical events.

The Kingdom of God is within us. Easter and Passover remind us that we have to let go in order to enter it. The space age demands that we change our ideas about ourselves, but we want to hold onto them. That's why there is a resurgence of old-fashioned orthodoxy in so many areas at the present time. There are no horizons in space, and there can be no horizons in our own experience. We cannot hold onto ourselves and our in-groups as we once did. The space age makes that possible, but people reject this demand or don't want to think about it. So they pull back into one true church or black power or the unions or the capitalist class.

Easter and Passover offer the perfect symbols, for they mean that we are called to new life. This new life is not very well defined, which is why we want to hold onto the past. The journey to this new life, a journey we all must make, cannot be made unless we let go of the past. The reality of living in space means that we are born anew; not born again to an old-time religion, but born to a new order of things: there are no horizons. That is the the meaning of the space age. We are in a free fall into a future that is mysterious. It is very fluid, and this is disconcerting to many people. All you have to do is know how to use a parachute.

St. Augustine speaks of Christ's going to the cross as a bridegroom to his bride. There is an affirmation here. In the Prado, there is a great painting by Titian of Simon of Cyrene as he willingly helps Jesus with the cross. The painting captures the free, human, voluntary participation we all must have in the Easter-Passover mystery. That is what we are all challenged to do. Self-preservation is only the second law of life. The first law is that you and the other are one.

173

IN Mark 13, Jesus says that the end of the world is going to come, and he describes it as a terrible crisis of fire and all kinds of other horrors. So, according to the teachings of the Catholic church, it's going to be a concrete historical event. And in Mark 13:30, Jesus says, "Amen I say to you, this generation will not pass away till all these things have been accomplished." But that generation did pass away, and the end of the world didn't come, so it's often called "the great nonevent." It didn't happen. So then the Catholic church said that when Jesus used the words "this generation," what he meant was the generation of mankind, and so this event is yet going to happen.

In the Thomas Gospel, on the other hand, when the apostles ask, "When will the Kingdom come?"—Jesus says, "The Kingdom will not come by expectation. They will not say 'see here, see there.' The Kingdom of the Father is spread upon the earth, and men do not see it."[100] That's Gnosticism.

> Gnosticism is the Western
> counterpart of Buddhism.

Thomas says, in other words, that there is a revelation possible to you right now. It is here. So, "to be happy with Him forever in heaven" means to reach that depth now. It's a totally different slant.

If you read Christian mythology
in the Gnostic way,
it makes universal sense.

Yet because the Catholic church insists that the coming of the Kingdom of the Father is going to be a historical event, every now and then, especially every thousand years, people think the end of the world is coming. In the year 1000, for instance, it was thought the end of the world was going to come, so people with a lot of property gave their property to the church to gain merit. There are still cases in the French courts to get that property back. Now it's time for the second millenium, so everyone is expecting annihilation. These expectations come automatically. There's always a way to envision that the end is going to happen. I do not know what the situation will be in the year 3000, but if any of you happen to be around in a later incarnation, you can expect that there will be some kind of panic.

You see, Christianity was born in a panic time. In the centuries just before the Christian era, the Levant was in turmoil. The Hellenistic empire was breaking up, Rome was in its ascendancy, and the Jewish community was in a hell of a condition.

In 167 B.C., Antiochus IV Epiphanes, the Seleucid emperor of Syria, installed a Greek altar on the Jewish altar in the temple court of Jerusalem. By establishing a Greek shrine in the Jewish temple compound, he hoped he would show that this religion was a variant of what all religions are about. No siree! Instead, Judas Maccabeus and his brothers killed the commissioner who was to establish the shrine. There was an uproar, the Maccabean revolt, which led to independent governance of the Jewish state for nearly a hundred years by a succession of Maccabean priest-kings.

In the age of the Maccabees the leaders in Jerusalem of the Hellenizing party were the Sadducees, among whom were priestly families claiming descent from the priestly patriarch Zadoc (Zadoc>Sadducee), and these were opposed chiefly by the Pharisees, or "Separatists," who believed themselves to be of a stricter orthodoxy—though, in fact, they had combined the old Hebrew heritage of a Day of Yahweh to come with the idea of the world end of Zoroastrian eschatology. [101]

During that period there was continual internecine conflict, which intensified in 104 B.C., when the Jewish king Aristobulus claimed that he was, essentially, also the Messiah. This was heresy! Though he reigned only a year, his son, Alexander Jannaeus, spent the next thirty fighting a series of wars and suppressing all Jewish insurrections with his foreign troops.

And with [his] death, 76 B.C., the Pharisees came to power, and the internecine tide only ran the other way. New purges, fratricides, betrayals, liquidations, and miracles kept the kingdom in uproar until, after a decade of such madness, the Roman legion of Pompey was invited by one of two brothers who were then contending for the crown to assist him in his holy cause; and it was in this way that the city of God, Jerusalem, passed in the year 63 B.C. into the sphere of Rome. [102]

It was a fantastic period in Jewish history. With all this going on, at least one sect, the Essenes, thought that the end of the world was coming. So, they went out near Wady Qumrân, at the northwest corner of the Dead Sea, and built a monastery, where they rigorously trained to survive that ultimate moment when the Messiah would appear. We've learned about this Essene community from the Dead Sea Scrolls, which were discovered hidden in desert caves and rock crannies. These fantastic documents exhibit a very strong Zoroastrian influence. Even some of the vocabulary is Zoroastrian. One of the scrolls, for example, projects detailed plans for a forty-year apocalyptic war between "the Sons of Light" and "the Sons of Darkness."

It is in this context, then, at precisely that time, the first century B.C., that St. John the Baptist was baptizing people only a few miles north of the Qumrân community. Now ritual bathing was a Qumrân rite, but John was not one of the Essenes, who wore white garments, for he wore the skins of animals and ate locusts and wild honey. The gospels recount that Jesus went out there, was baptized by John, and then went into the desert to have his own experience, known as "the Temptation in the Desert." After forty days in the desert—imitating, in small, the Hebrew's forty years—he returned and began to teach. And that's where his story really begins.

It is not dissimilar from the story of the Buddha, who also goes out, studies with the principle teachers of the time, goes beyond them in his austerities, comes to illumination, and returns. Whether or not it happened to either of them is a question. The myth of a teacher who goes past all teachers is a standard motif.

What Jesus thought he was, we just don't know. He didn't write anything. He talked sometimes as though he thought he was the god of the Greek mysteries who dies and is resurrected—dies to today and is resurrected to tomorrow—but he wrote, as it were, in sand. What little we do know about him, we've learned from the four gospels, and they are of different dates and actually differ considerably. For instance, if you look in your Bible, you will see that the Virgin Birth motif is found only in the gospel of Luke, a Greek. In Matthew and Mark, where the genealogy of Jesus is related in detail from David on down the royal line, it ends up, not with Mary, but with Joseph. Though we do not know the date of Jesus' birth—we know nothing about it, in fact, except what we read in Luke—if he died, he probably died around 30 A.D. The gospels are funny things. They don't agree. Unfortunately, four people wrote them, and they wrote differing accounts.

Luke seems to have traveled with Paul, and the earliest writings about Jesus are those of Paul, who never saw him. Paul, in fact, was in the crowd of Jewish zealots who killed the first Christian martyr, St. Stephen—which, by the way, is why Joyce calls his hero Stephen Dedalus. It was shortly after that event, on the road to Damascus, that Paul's conversion took place: he had a vision, fell off his horse, and, so to speak, "founded Christianity." It seems that Paul, a Jew who wrote elegant Greek, was torn between the monotheistic culture of Judaism and the non-dualistic Greek tradition. So, my notion of what happened to Paul is that he realized that the catastrophic killing of this young, inspired Jewish rabbi could be read as an enactment of the death and resurrection of the Greek mystery hero.

Now, monotheism is a concretization of God, a mystery that actually transcends concretization, and the concretization of the mystery savior in Jesus is equivalent. So, God is concretized, the savior is concretized, the end of the world is concretized, and Christianity loses its metaphoric perspective. If you read the historical "facts" as metaphors, however, then you will discover in Christianity a marvelous array of psychologically valid symbols that are fundamentally okay until they're concretized.

Concretization is alright for teaching little children, who don't understand metaphor. Matters such as these, they tend to take concretely. What has to happen at a certain point in one's development is that these childhood concretizations have to be opened up. You can't get rid of them, because symbols that are taken concretely are put right into you. They are internalized and can't just be dismissed. They have to be reread. I know. Until I was twenty-five-years old I took Christianity concretely. And I must say I'm grateful for having been exposed to such rich symbolism.

Yet there's also some great strength to be gained by giving up that religion, by going beyond it. I mean, if you really do. If you just "drop out," that's something else. But if you think it through—if you learn to read the symbols as metaphors instead of accepting them as the facts they're purported to be—if you know, in other words, why you are out, then it can be a source of great strength. But when you do break out, you then have to set up your own sacred field.

When I was student, still in the Catholic church, there was one week each year when we gave up all our studies and spent our time listening to sermons: some were like the hell sermon Joyce recounts in *A Portrait of the Artist as a Young Man*; others were on such themes as the meaning of the sacraments. The purpose of these "retreats," as they were called, was to remove us from the secular world and put us in a sacred space.

Such events are examples of the church creating a sacred space, but it's the *church's* sacred space, set up according to its program. Now, if the church is the rope you're hanging onto, if that is what's bringing you to your bliss place, then this approach avoids the problem of working this stuff out for yourself. But another way is to have your own little tabernacle, your own sacred space, from which you exclude everything else.

A sacred space is any space that is set apart from the usual context of life. In the secular context, one is concerned with pairs of opposites: cause and effect, gain and loss, and so on. Sacred space has no function in the way of earning a living or a reputation. Practical use is not the dominant feature of anything in the space. You do not have anything in your sacred space that's not of significance to you for the harmonization of your own life. In your sacred space, things are working in terms of *your* dynamic—and not anybody else's.

> Your sacred space is
> where you can find yourself
> again and again.

You really don't have a sacred space, a rescue land, until you find somewhere to be that's not a wasteland, some field of action where there is a spring of ambrosia —a joy that comes from inside, not something external that puts joy into you— a place that lets you experience your own will and your own intention and your own wish so that, in small, the Kingdom is there. I think everybody, whether they know it or not, is in need of such a place.

Sacred space and sacred time and something joyous to do is all we need. Almost anything then becomes a continuous and increasing joy.

> What you have to do,
> you do with play.

I think a good way to conceive of sacred space is as a playground. If what you're doing seems like play, you are in it. But you can't play with my toys, you have to have your own. Your life should have yielded some. Older people play with life experiences and realizations or with thoughts they like to entertain. In my case, I have books I like to read that don't lead anywhere.

> One great thing about growing old
> is that nothing
> is going to lead to anything.
> Everything is of the moment.

When Jung decided to try to discover the myth by which he was living, he asked himself, "What was the game I enjoyed when I was a child?" His answer was making little towns and streets out of stones. So, he bought some property and, as a way of playing, began to build a house. It was a lot of work, utterly unnecessary for he already had a house, but an appropriate way to create sacred space. It was sheer play.

> What did you do as a child
> that created timelessness,
> that made you forget time?

> There lies the myth to live by.

What do you like to do? What have you learned to do? Jung was a big, strong man, and he liked to push rocks around, so that's what he did. I'll bet that if you search back, you'll find connections between the sacred space that you have now and a really special space that you had as a child.

> As an adult,
> you must rediscover
> the moving power of your life.
>
> Tension, a lack of honesty,
> and a sense of unreality
> come from following
> the wrong force in your life.

In my own situation, when I was between the ages of about eleven and fifteen, I was crazy about American Indians. My family bought me *The Complete Works of Parkman*, reports of the Bureau of Ethnology, and all sorts of other books on the subject. I had a very nice little library, with beautiful, bronze, Indian heads that were bookends, and Navajo rugs, and so on. Then the house burned down. It was a terrible crisis in our family. My grandmother was killed. All of my things were gone.

I now realize that the sacred space I created for myself, the room in which I do my writing, is really a reconstruction—a reactivation, if you will—of my boyhood space. When I go in there to write, I'm surrounded by books that have helped me to find my way, and I recall moments of reading certain works that were particularly insightful. When I sit down to do the writing, I pay close attention to little ritual details —where the notepads and pencils are placed, that sort of thing—so that everything is exactly as I remember it having been before. It's all a sort of "set-up" that releases me. And since that space is associated with a certain kind of performance, it evokes that performance again. But the performance is play.

> Work begins
> when you don't like
> what you're doing.

And if your life isn't play, or if you are engaged in play and having no fun, well, quit! The spirit of the sacred space is Shiva dancing. All responsibilities are cast off. There are various ways of doing this casting off. and it doesn't matter how it happens. The rest is play.

"Any man who is attached to the senses and things of this world...is one who lives in ignorance and is being consumed by the snakes that represent his own passions." —Black Elk[103]

A sacred space is hermetically sealed off from the temporal world. When you're in such a space, there is no penetration through the enclosure. You are in an eternal zone that is protected from the impact of the stimuli of the day and the hour. That's what you do in meditation: seal yourself off. The meditation posture is a sealing-off posture, and the regularized breathing furthers your inward-turned explorations. The world is sealed off, and you become a self-contained entity.

You must have such a sealing-off program for yourself whenever you require it: once a week, once a day, or once an hour. Of what value is that? It is an absolute necessity if you are going to have an inner life. What it provides is an interval in which the eternal within you is disengaged from the field of time. We spoke earlier of God's making us "to know Him, to love Him, and to serve Him in this world," *out there*, "and to be happy with him forever in heaven," in the hermetically sealed sacred space *within yourself*. The further you can get into that, the more at peace you will be with whatever happens.

I was thinking of the sorts of conditions you set up for yourself to achieve the visit to the Grail Castle—for that's what this sacred space is: the place where your associations are not with the field of phenomenal experience, but with the field of your own inward life. You do not get there in the normal run of life. To visit the Grail Castle, you have to have a sacred space. Then, once you have found the connection in your sacred space, you can perhaps translate it into other parts of your life. But first you have to have a little oil well, as it were, that goes down deep.

> To live in sacred space
> is to live in a symbolic environment
> where spiritual life is possible,
> where everything around you
> speaks of exaltation of the spirit.

I've been traveling a lot the last ten years, and when I'm not somewhere I've been before, the kind of hotel room I prefer is a completely noncommittal room, an efficient room, the kind you find in a Holiday Inn. I open my bag, put my books on the table, hang my clothes on the open rack, and that's it: here is Joe Campbell and here are his books—so what more do we have in the world? You can turn any place into a sacred space once you have your own sacred space. However, you can say that sacred space is everywhere only after you have learned, through a meditation discipline or the experience of sacred places, what the sanctity is. It is the metaphoric relevance of the object.

> In sacred space,
> everything is done
> so that the environment
> becomes a metaphor.

In India, I've seen sacred places that are just a red circle put around a stick or a stone in such a way that the environment becomes metaphoric: when you look at that stick or stone, you see it as a manifestation of Brahman, a manifestation of the mystery.

Sacred space is a space that is transparent to transcendence, and everything within such a space furnishes a base for meditation. I'm thinking specifically of those Indian temples with a great wall around them: when you enter through the door, everything within that space is symbolic, the whole world is mythologized.

The earliest sacred spaces of which we have any evidence might well have been the little shrines of Neanderthal man, where there was a cave-bear skull and a lighted fire to build up a little atmosphere. The first, real sacred spaces were probably caves in southern France and northern Spain, dating from 30,000 B.C. When you go into those caves, you are in a magical sacred space, and your consciousness is transformed. I remember going into the big cave in Lascaux. It was fantastic. That universe down there seemed to be the primary world. The animals above ground were simply reflections of those on the walls of the caves. You don't want to leave a place like that. The majesty and magic of it all somehow brings you into your own center. And once you are there, then sacred space is everywhere.

I've been a few places like that where I've thought, "A breakthrough is possible here. This is a place for the exercises that will bring me to where I want to be." That's the whole meaning of a cult. A cult is a sacred place. But if you get stuck in a cult—if you think, "I just can't be anywhere if I'm not here"—well, that's too bad. You're still in training.

WHEN I was in India, I wanted to meet a real, first-class master, and I didn't want to hear any more slop about *maya* and how you've got to give up the world and all that kind of thing. I'd had enough of that for about fifteen or twenty years. I was nosing around, listening, and I heard of one master in Trivandrum, in southwest India, and I decided to go see him. His mystic name was "Sri Atmananda." I'll call him that. Now when you get close to a master of that kind, you're bound to meet a lot of nuts. You just are, there's no doubt about it. But I knew that if I went, and if I was on the beam, I would get to see him.

I went to this funny little hotel called the Mascot Hotel, where all the rooms opened out onto a veranda. It was fiercely hot, and I was seated on the veranda, when this chap comes up to me without any introduction, shows me this great big watch, and says, "See that? I have an hour hand, and I have a minute hand, and I have a second hand. " Before I can respond, he says, "Men have periods, just as women do, only they don't know it. But I've worked mine out. It's represented on this watch." I looked at the watch. On it were two little scales, a red and white one on one side and a black and white one on the other, with little indicators that could go this way or that. He points to the red and white scale and says, "When this hand is over on the red side, I'm in my period. When it is in the white, I'm out." Then pointing to the other scale, he says, "We have mental periods also, and I have those worked out too. When this hand is on the black and the other is on the red, I stay home." Imagine what it cost him to have that thing made.

That evening, down in the dining room, I saw a man and woman, who looked like translucent praying mantises. They were seated just across the room, and between them, on the table, was a tall vase, and it was filled with food that they took out and ate with their fingers. Later I met the man and learned that he was president of the International Vegetarian Society. He said he had come to India to reform vegetarianism, that the Indian people didn't know anything about it! At the next table, two gentlemen were talking, and I heard one of them mention the name "Arthur Gregor." Now, I knew a young American poet with that name, and I knew that he was in India, so I said, "Pardon me, did I hear you mention Arthur Gregor?" They said, "Yes, he is with Sri Atmananda." I said, "Would you give him my regards? My name is Joseph Campbell."

Two days later, I was invited to meet the guru. If you're on your right track, that's the way it goes: doors open miraculously. So, I went to a lovely cottage, and at the door was an Indian with a long, white beard. He said, "The master is upstairs." I went up to an attic that was perfectly naked except for two chairs. Atmananda was seated in one, and I was to sit in the other, facing him. I mean, it was a real confrontation.

He said, "Do you have a question?" I had the good fortune, I later learned, to ask exactly the question that had been his first question to *his* guru, so we had a very good conversation. When we'd concluded, he said he had now to go down to his class. He dismissed me, and I thanked him. Now, I had made arrangements to meet some members of that class in a coffee shop after the class was finished. When I came in, one of them said, "The master said you are on the brink of illumination." Why? Because of the question I had asked.

My question was this: "Since all is Brahman, all is the divine radiance, how can we say 'no' to ignorance or brutality or anything?" His answer was: "For you and me, we say 'yes.'"

> Breaking the ideals of society
> is the path of the mystic.

Then he gave me a little meditation: "Where are you between two thoughts?" That is to say, you are thinking all the time, and you have an image of yourself. Well, where are you between two thoughts? Do you ever have a glimpse beyond your thinking of that which transcends anything you can think about yourself? *That's* the source field out of which all of your energies are coming.

> In meditating,
> meditate on your own divinity.
>
> The goal of life is to be a vehicle
> for something higher.
>
> Keep your eye up there
> between the pairs of opposites
> watching your *play* in the world.
>
> Let the world be as it is
> and learn to rock with the waves.
>
> Remain "radiant,"
> as Joyce put it,
> in the filth of the world.

A Buddha image is not a picture of the historical Buddha. We are all Buddha beings, all things are Buddha beings. So, an image of the Buddha is not a graven image to be understood concretely. It is a meditation tool, something to be seen *through*. It is a support for meditation on the Buddhahood within you, not a depiction of any actual Buddha "out there."

God and Buddhas in the Orient are not final terms like Yahweh, the Trinity, or Allah, in the West—but point beyond themselves to that ineffable being, consciousness, and rapture that is the All in all of us. And in their worship, the ultimate aim is to effect in the devotee a psychological transfiguration through a shift of his plane of vision from the passing to the enduring, through which he may come finally to realize in experience (not simply as an act of faith) that he is identical with that before which he bows. [104]

> The entire heavenly realm
> is within us, but to find it
> we have to relate to what's outside.

It is in this context that one says, "If you see the Buddha coming down the road, kill him." That is to say, if your notion of Buddhahood is concretized to that extent, then cancel the concretization. You cannot say that about Jesus, at least not in the orthodoxy.

You must kill your god.

If you are to advance,
all fixed ideas must go.

Most Buddhas that one sees depicted are what are known as "meditation Buddhas," and they never lived. They represent Buddha powers within all of us, and in contemplating them, you will choose and be guided by your own Buddha—as, in the Catholic tradition, your principle guide is a particular saint, who represents virtues and qualities that are somehow accessible to you. The Buddha image, then, isn't a picture of the Buddha. It is a tool to help you meditate on the Buddhahood within yourself.

This whole drift of Buddhism comes to a very clean expression in Zen, where there are no images. The only picture in a Zen monastery would be of Bodhidharma, the wall-gazing teacher who came to China from India, and that image would simply be a reminder of how to meditate. Finding the Buddha within yourself is a difficult exercise, and sometimes images help. You have to realize that Buddhism is not only an elite religion, but also a popular religion. A popular religion must provide bases for meditation. As a result, there is a long history in Buddhism of relic worship. All of those great *stupas*, those monuments of the early Buddhist world, are reliquary mounds. Each one contains a relic, just as every Catholic church is supposed to be built on a relic. It is all a base for meditation.

Two great divisions of Buddhist thinking are distinguished. The first was dedicated to the ideal of individual salvation and represented the way to this end as monastic self-discipline. The second, which seems to have matured in northern India during and following the first and second centuries A.D. (long after the other had been disseminated as far southward as the island of Ceylon), proposed the ideal of salvation for all and developed disciplines of popular devotion and universal secular service. The earlier is known as the Hīnayāna, "the lesser or little (hīna) boat or vehicle (yāna)," while the second is the Mahāyāna, "the great (mahat) boat or vehicle," the boat in which all can ride.[105]

Before the period of Mahāyāna Buddhism, the Buddha was never depicted. Hence, in the illustration of the Buddha's life on the early *stūpas,* there are only symbols of the Buddha—his footprints, an umbrella, a sun disk—because the Buddha is one who is identified no longer with his ego but with total consciousness, and consequently, cannot be depicted. He's like the sun that has set, and you don't depict what is not. As a result, in early depictions of the Temptation of the Buddha, the temptation is rendered—on one side of the throne are the posturing daughters of *Kāma,* Lord Desire, and on the other, the ogres of *Māra,* King Death—but nobody is in the throne. Well, there *was* nobody there. He was not identified with this personality.

With the arrival of Mahāyāna, however, comes the idea that the distinction between *nirvāṇa* and *saṁsāra* —"the round of being," the round of rebirth—is a dualism, and the two are, in fact, one: *nirvāṇa* is here, this is it. There is a total transformation of consciousness, and images of the Buddha appear. Images of everything appear, because they are all Buddha things.

The word *saṁsāra* refers to the torrent of time, to our participation in the Dionysian passage of time with all things coming and going. Time explodes forms and brings out new ones, and you are one of those forms. In so far as you identify with your body, you think, "Oh, my God, here I go!" You live in life; you die; and, depending on your life, you go either to a hell or a heaven, and from there you come back to the next life. In the Oriental system, this is all *saṁsāra,* the round of being. *Nirvāṇa* goes past that. We are but reflections on the wall of the cave. From where do they come?

The word *nirvāṇa* means "blown out," the breath that enlivens the world has been blown out of you. In Jainism, another Indian philosophy, *nirvāṇa* is thought of as death. But in Indian there is reincarnation, so you cannot truly die until you've achieved release from life.

The Buddha is the one who stresses the psychological aspect of this "dying." You can stay alive, in action, but be disengaged from desire for, and fear of, the fruits of your actions. This psychological disengagement of your passions from the events of your life is *nirvāṇa.*

With the Mahāyāna, then, comes the simultaneous experience of these two attitudes toward the one thing which is life. So, you can be alive, in saṁsāra, but acting without passion—that's *nirvāṇa.* That's also the idea in the post-Buddhistic *Bhagavad Gita*, 563–483 B.C.

> The *Bhagavad Gita* says:
> "Get in there and do your thing.
> Don't worry about the outcome."
>
> Recognize sorrow as of the essence.
> When there is time, there is sorrow.
>
> We can't rid the world of sorrow,
> but we can choose to live in joy.

The term bodhisattva, "one whose being (sattva) is enlightenment (bodhi)," had been employed in the earlier vocabulary...to designate one on the way to realization but not yet arrived: a Buddha in his earlier lives, a Future Buddha. In the new vocabulary...the term was used to represent the sage who, while living in the world, has refused the boon of cessation yet achieved realization, and so remains a perfect knower in the world as a beacon, guide, and compassionate savior of all beings.[106]

The Bodhisattva voluntarily
comes back into the world
knowing that it's a mess.

He doesn't come back
"only if it's sweet for me."

The Bodhisattva
participates joyfully
in the sorrows of the world.

"The great Mahāyāna Bodhisattva Avalokiteshvara is a personification of the highest ideal of the Mahāyāna Buddhist career. His legend recounts that when, following a series of eminently virtuous incarnations, he was about to enter into the surcease of nirvāṇa, an uproar, like the sound of a general thunder, rose in all the worlds. The great being knew that this was a wail of lament uttered by all created things—the rocks and stones as well as the trees, insects, gods, animals, demons, and human beings of all the spheres of the universe—at the prospect of his imminent departure from the realms of birth. And so, in his compassion, he renounced for himself the boon of nirvāṇa until all beings without exception should be prepared to enter in before him—like the good shepherd

who permits his flock to pass first through the gate and then goes through himself, closing it behind him."—Zimmer[107]

The Bodhisattva Avalokiteshvara, with a woman's earring in one ear and a man's in the other, represents mercy, or compassion. The name Avalokiteshvara is a difficult word to translate, but the sense of it is "he who looks down on the world with mercy." Avalokiteshvara is frequently pictured as a male flanked by two female figures called "Taras," personifications of the tears of mercy that flow from the Bodhisattva's eyes: one from the right eye, the other from the left. The word *tara* is related to our word "star" and to the verb "to strew." The Taras strew out mercy to the world, which is, to me, one of the most darling notions.

When this tradition went to the Far East, to China and Japan, Avalokiteshvara's feminine aspects were accented and this Bodhisattva became female, represented in the character of Kuan-yin, Kwannon in Japanese, for the female form was thought to be a more appropriate manifestation of the fostering of self-giving compassion than the male, which usually represents discipline.

Peace is at the heart of all because Avalokiteshvara-Kwannon, the mighty Bodhisattva, Boundless Love, includes, regards, and dwells within (without exception) every sentient being. The perfection of the delicate wings of an insect, broken in the passage of time, he regards—and he himself is both their perfection and their disintegration.[108]

In another manifestation, Avalokiteshvara has a thousand hands surrounding him like a halo, and in the palm of each is an eye that is pierced by the sorrows of the world, as Christ's hands were pierced by nails. They are equivalent symbols. Christ is a Bodhisattva. Buddhists have no problem accepting Christ, but they don't accept him as a unique manifestation and the only way.

Mahāyāna Buddhism and Christianity grew up simultaneously. The two systems are of the same dates and developed fifteen-hundred miles apart on a military road that was built by the Persians.

When the Bodhisattva teaches, we have been told, he assumes the outward forms of his auditors; but his message is addressed to the Wisdom-Self within each, to wake and call it to life.[109]

When the Dalai Lama, the incarnation of Avalokiteshvara, first came to New York, there was an interesting event. At his first reception, in St. Patrick's Cathedral—where there were Roman Catholic clergy, Eastern patriarchs, Jewish rabbis, and, I suppose, even psychiatrists—what he said was, "All of your ways are valid ways to expansion of consciousness and illumination." Of course, Cardinal Cook had to get up and say, "No, we're different. Our religion is not to be confused with these other ways."

I was also at the next event, a Buddhist event at the Cathedral of St. John the Divine. About fifteen-hundred people from various Buddhist communities or societies in New York gathered in the big nave of that cathedral and had a real Tibetan ceremony, with monks chanting and all. The Dahli Lama gave a brief talk in Tibetan and a young man instantly translated his intricate theological Tibetan into English. What a fantastic performance!

What the Dalai Lama said was, "Now you are on the Buddhist way. Keep up your meditation, as there is no instant illumination. The mind moves slowly into this. Do not become attached to *your* method. When, in the course of your meditation, your consciousness will have expanded and been transformed, you will then recognize that all the ways are valid ways."

> The rational mind
> stresses opposites.
>
> Compassion and love
> go beyond pairs of opposites.

The Bodhisattva Manjushri is shown with a sword known as "the sword of discrimination." Discrimination has to do with discriminating between the mortal and the eternal. The mortal is that which you see. When you see yourself in the mirror, that is the mortal. The eternal is that which you are. So, discriminating in your life between the eternal and the mortal is the essence of this figure.

> The sword is usually
> a benevolent instrument
> which clears the way.

When you are desiring things and fearing things, that's mortality. The three temptations of the Buddha —desire, fear, and duty—are what hold you in the field of time. When you put the hermetic seal around yourself and, by discriminating between the mortal and the enduring, you find that still place within yourself that does not change, that's when you've achieved *nirvāṇa*. That still point is the firmly burning flame that is not rippled by any wind.

When you find that burning flame within yourself, action becomes facilitated in athletics, in playing a musical piece on the piano, or in performance of any kind.. If you can hold to that still place within yourself while engaged in the field, your performance will be masterly. That's what the Samurai does. And the real athlete.

Watch a professional marathon runner: he is not concerned with his showing the way somebody who is running his first race is. You win, you lose, you run the race. The race is what counts, not the winning or the losing. Running the marathon is itself the event. Everybody wins. Whether you win or place is a secondary matter. This is participation without engagement.

But if you lose that still point, you are all in the world. If, for example, you go into the race as a front runner, thinking you are going to have to win, and you are concerned that you don't quite have the capacity to do so, then you won't be participating in the marathon. Nietzsche says one must act with only three-quarters of one's power. That's the discrimination.

> Anything you do has a still point.
> When you are in that still point,
> you can perform maximally.

Where are you between two thoughts? If you identify yourself with certain actions, certain achievements and failures, those are thoughts. That's you in the field of time and experience. Where are you otherwise?

If it weren't difficult to get to that still point, there wouldn't have to be so much talk about it and all this sitting in postures trying to get there. And then, when you get up from the posture, you are right back where you were. So, you go back to the posture to see if you can get there again. It's not easy; yet, it's very easy. It's like riding a bicycle: you keep falling off until you know how to ride, and then you can't fall off.

It's a perspective problem. Running through the field of time is this energy which is the one energy that is putting itself into all these forms. By identifying with that one energy, you are at the same time indentified with the forms coming and going. If you see the two modes—involvement and the still point within you, *saṁsāra* and *nirvāṇa*—as separate from each other, you are in a dualistic position. But when you realize that the two are one, you can hold to your still point while engaging. It's the same world experienced in two different ways. You can experience both ways at once.

Sri Ramkrishna was devoted to the Goddess Kali. Kali, the word means "black" and also "time," is that black abyss of mystery out of which all things come and back into which they go. That's Kali. Her principle image is that of dancing in the burning ground,the place where corpses are burned. This is dissolution. She is dancing on the body of her god, Shiva, her husband. Your god is the final obstacle to get past.

Any idea, any concept, any name, is a final obstacle. The one preached in the church in any religion is the final obstacle. The only Western teacher I have found who gets it is Meister Eckhart, who says, "The ultimate leave-taking is the leaving of God for God." All of our religions hang onto the image. None has gone past its god. The still point is going past the god. Goethe says, "Everything temporal is but a symbol."[110] Nietzsche says, "Everything eternal is but a metaphor." They are saying the same thing. "Everything" includes God, heaven, hell, the whole works. So as long as you are living to get to heaven, you won't find that still place.

> One has to go beyond
> the pairs of opposites
> to find the real source.

In Buddhism, those who attain *nirvāṇa* are said to have "achieved the yonder shore"; that is to say, they have crossed the river from the normal experience of life to the yonder shore of *nirvāṇa*, beyond all pairs of opposites, beyond twoness. Heinrich Zimmer gave this amusing anecdote to help us understand Buddhism:

Let's say you're living in San Francisco, and you are simply fed up with San Francisco. You have heard of Berkeley: the wonderful people there and these councils of sages. There are domes that suggest temples. You've never been to such a place, but you have heard of it. It seems that this Berkeley would be a great escape from San Francisco, and so—in the old days before the bridge —you go to the shore, you look across, and you think, "If I could only get away from this place—*saṁsāra,* the world of pain and effort—and go to Berkeley, I would be saved."

Well, one fine day, you see a ferryboat set off from the yonder shore, and it comes right to where you are standing. There's a man in the boat who says, "Anyone for Berkeley?" This is the Buddha in the Buddha boat. And you say, "I." And he says, "Well, get aboard, but remember: this is a one-way trip. It takes great effort. There's no coming back to San Francisco. You will give up everything: your career, your family, your ambitions. Everything." You say, "I'm fed up with everything." "Okay," he says, "you are eligible."

This ferryboat is known as the "lesser vehicle." It's for "Little Ferryboat" Buddhism, Monk Buddhism. To board it, you have to be ready to become a monk or a nun and give up the whole thing. In India, the saffron robes the monks wear are the color of the garment put on a corpse. These men are dead. Are you ready to put on the garment of a corpse? You are? Get on the boat.

Sri Ramakrishna says,
"Do not seek illumination
unless you seek it
as a man whose hair is on fire
seeks a pond."

The ferryboat starts out, and it suddenly comes over you what you're leaving, but you are already on the boat. You're a monk or a nun. You're a sailor. You love the sound of the waves slapping on the side of the boat, you learn how to lift sails and bring them down, and you use a different vocabulary: you call the right side, the "starboard" side, and the left side, the "port"; the front is "fore," the back, "aft." You don't know any more about Berkeley than you did before you got on the boat, but people in San Francisco you're now calling "fools." You thought it would be a short trip, but it may continue for three or four incarnations.

This is the monk's life. This is the student's life. This is obeying orders. Life is reduced to pushing beads here and there and chanting OM. You have reduced life to something that is a pretty simple affair. You would not want that to end. It's like a situation I've seen in art studios: the student is working on a piece of sculpture, and the master looks at it and says, "Continue." Of course, the disaster would be if he said, "You've got it, you're finished." "Oh no, I don't want to leave school." The last thing you want is not to be a monk or a nun.

Finally, after several incarnations, the boat scrapes ashore, and you think, "This is it: rapture, *nirvāṇa*!" You go ashore. There are explosions: LSD and the whole goddamn thing—but it's not the goal at all.

The Buddha, in the conversations known as the "Medium-length Dialogues," says, "Oh, Monks, supposing a man, wishing to get to the yonder shore, should build himself a raft, and by virtue of that raft, achieve the yonder shore; then, out of gratitude for the raft, he picks it up and carries it about on his shoulder. Would that be an intelligent man?" The monks reply, "No, Master, that would not be an intelligent man." "So," says the Buddha, "the laws and experiences of the order of yoga have nothing to do with *nirvāṇa*. The vehicle of the doctrine is the way that you get to the yonder shore, and having attained it, you cast away the raft and forsake it."

So, you are on the yonder shore, and you think, "I wonder how San Francisco looks from Berkeley?" You turn around and...there is no San Francisco, there is no bay, there is no boat, there is no Buddha.

You thought there was an opposition. You were still thinking in terms of pairs of opposites. The place you have left is exactly where you are. It's simply your perspective that has been changed. This is the point of view of the so-called "Great Ferryboat," or Mahāyāna tradition, where we realize that all things are Buddha things, we are on the Great Ferryboat, and the ferryboat is already there. Furthermore, since the first doctrine of Buddhism is "no self," there is nobody on the boat! The real self is that transcendent life and Buddha consciousness of which we are all just visionary moments. This is the Mahāyāna.

So we hear next, "Delight is yoga." The life you are living is your yoga. As Ramakrishna put it, "The little nephew that you love is your God." The irony of this wonderful discipline is that it teaches that you, who were bored, are in exactly the same place, but in rapture, simply because you've shifted your level of consciousness. You've given up thinking things should be the way they are not, and you realize, "This is it. This is it. This is it." And you get to saying "This is it" by first saying, "This is *not* it." That discrimination forces you into a different level of consciousness. What "isn't it" is the way you're looking at it.

> The Buddha is the one whose eye
> of full consciousness has opened.

This is the journey that comes through worship, because a deity represents a degree of power, a degree of consciousness of knowledge and love that is on a level not immediately apparent to the eyes. The Tantric saying "to worship a god, you must become a god" means you must find in yourself the level of consciousness and love that the deity epitomizes and symbolizes. When you do, you are worshiping that deity.

It doesn't matter what name you give the deity. People say, "Oh, we are Christians: Father, Son, Holy Ghost, and the Virgin Mary." But if you can't get into yourself on the level of the Christ within you, you are not a Christian. And depending on the level of awareness you have reached, your worship will be different from that of people in the same church who aren't at the same level. Saying you are a member of this church, that church, or the other is a social notion, a sociological phenomenon that has nothing to do with religion.

What is your religion telling you?
How to be a Jew? A Catholic?
Or how to be a human being?

I had a friend, a marvelous young man named John, who became an editor of the Jesuit periodical *America* about the time that the Catholic church got interested in the ecumenical movement. Everybody was trying to correlate Catholicism with the other religions, but at the same time, they were denigrating them. So, John would always be telling them, for example, "No, you can't do that with Hinduism. You can't put it down by misrepresenting it. You've got to face up to it."

Well, there was a big Roman Catholic conference of the meditation orders—Cistercians, Trappists, and so forth—in Bangkok, and John was there as an observer. By the way, it was while attending this conference that Thomas Merton died. He was electrocuted by a bad fixture in some absurd Thai hotel. John later said that the talk that Merton had given just before his death was one of the most magnificent he'd ever heard.

When John came back, he said the Christian monks and Buddhist monks had no problem communicating. As anyone who's tried to be a poet knows, when you've had a spiritual experience, the words don't render it. All they can do is give a clue. The experience goes beyond anything that can be said. The religious sense is implied in the metaphoric language of religion. "But," he said, "the lay clergy who have never had the experience, but have only read the books, *are in collision all the time*."

What is the Kingdom?

It lies in our realization of the ubiquity
of the divine presence in our neighbors,
in our enemies, in all of us.[111]

$\mathbf{T}$he big lesson in Buddhism, then, the sense of what we have been saying is, "Get away from your rational system and get into the wonderful experience that is moving through all things all the time."

It is through living
that we experience and communicate
the spirit.

It is through life
that we learn to live in the spirit.

One in full quest of the spirit
knows that the goal of life is death.

I recall a wonderful talk I had with Alan Watts, who was a marvelous man. One of my problems was that Jean was always late. I'd make an appointment to meet her somewhere or other, and there I'd sit waiting for half-an-hour. I found it's a normal thing for men to wait for women. They have so many things they have to do before they can walk out of the house that half-an-hour or more goes by quickly.

Now, it's a basic rule in New York that it takes a half-hour to get anywhere, but Jean always thought that the time when she was supposed to be somewhere was the time to leave. So, I had this long wait problem, and I said to Alan, "What can I do about this? I get aggravated, and when she arrives, I'm a little bit nasty."

Alan said, "Well, your problem is that you want her to be there, and you're wishing for a situation that is not the one you are in. Just realize that you are ruining the experience that you could be having there while waiting by thinking it should be otherwise."

So then, waiting for Jean became a spiritual exercise. I said to myself, "You should not be thinking that Jean should be here. Look around you and see what is going on." And, you know, the place where I was became so goddamn interesting that I wasn't bored at all. Oftentimes, I hoped that Jean would make me wait a little longer. That would have seemed impossible to me, until Alan suggested shutting out any thought that my situation should have been otherwise.

That's an example of what fear and desire do. I desired the situation to be the one we planned, and that desire forbade me my immediate experience: "This is it! This is life! Look at it! Isn't it bubbling?" But now that I could love the situation I was in, the waiting was no longer a bore. The psychological transformation would be that whatever was formerly endured is now known, loved, and served.

> As long as you move
> from a place of fear and desire,
> you are self-excluded
> from immortality.

The aim of all religious exercises is a psychological transformation. You can make up your own meditations and rites based on knowing, loving, and serving the deity in caring for your children, doctoring drunks, or writing books. Any work whatsoever can be a meditation if you have the sense that everything is Brahman: the process, the doing, the thing that is being looked at, the one that is looking—everything.

> The return
> is seeing the radiance
> everywhere.

The main problem is changing the location of your mind. The town you come back to is the one you left, otherwise the journey is not complete. You come back to whatever you regard as the place that is your life, to the same carreer, not necessarily to the same locale. The yoga disciplines *are* disciplines. They are not the place.

> You give yourself to life
> by leaving temporality behind.

> Desire for mortal gains
> and fear of loss
> hold you back from giving
> yourself to life.

Fear and desire do not give rise to social duty, society does. Do-gooders come and say, for example, "We have this picket line against nuclear armament. Please get on the line, give up your thinking, and do what we ask you to do."

> If you're performing your social duty,
> it is not *your* act at all.
> Society has put it upon you
> and it will keep you from life.

Dealing with such demands as compulsory social obligations means you are linked and locked to a given order of life in the phenomenal world. You can involve yourself voluntarily, but there is no compulsion upon you to participate in these actions. Nor are they necessarily the final good of mankind. That's the whole didactic sphere.

People put social duty on you. Your neighbors say, "Why this apathetic sitting in meditation? Get up and do something for the world. You owe it to the world." All that kind of thing. Duty doesn't rise out of your fear. People put it on you. Duty is dharma; that is to say, dharma understood as social dharma.

Notice that little icon on the dollar bill, the static eye at the point where the pair of opposites come together. If you're going to be in the world in action, you have to be down the pyramid on one side or the other. It doesn't matter whether you are for Democracy or Communism or Fascism, you are still in the field of time, and the radiance shines through no matter which one you're in. You can also get locked into compulsive participation in any position. It is a matter of relativity. All judgments are transformed as you move from one position to another. Good and evil are not absolute. They are relative to which side you are on.

> The limitation comes
> where your judgment comes.

A wonderful example is a story I was told about a Buddhist monk whom a friend was following. Now in

Tibet, people go to a slaughter-house, buy a lamb that is about to be killed, then give the lamb its freedom, and that is a pious act. Accordingly, this monk, who had a cluster of beautiful girls around him, was going to perform a pious act by freeing five hundred fish.

And so, with his constellation of beauties, he went from one bait shop to another in Monterey trying to buy five hundred minnows. But bait was in short supply, and the shopkeepers said they were not going to sell him minnows for liberation. Finally, however, he found a shop that would, and he and his entourage, carrying buckets filled with fish, went down to the shore, where they had a ceremony of blessing the fish that were about to be given their freedom. Then they dumped one bucket after another into the ocean. Well, pelicans flocked from every point of the compass, and the little monk ran back and forth, waving his robe, trying to keep the pelicans away.

Now, what is good for pelicans is bad for fish, and this monk had taken sides. He was not in the middle place. This is to me a very important story. Every now and then, I wake up laughing at that monk and his banquet for the pelicans.

That is why the story of the lion lying down with the lamb is so silly. Read concretely, you realize that when the lion is eating the lamb, he is lying down with it. That's how it was meant to be, and "shanti, shanti, shanti": nothing is happening. That is the perspective of the sublime, which annihilates ego consciousness and its relationship. Without changing the world, there is escape from sorrow just by shifting the perspective.

Life will always be sorrowful.

We can't change it, but we can change our attitude toward it.

There is a story of the Buddha, in a little company of yogis, and he says, "At one time I starved my body to such a degree that, when I touched my stomach, I could grab my backbone. The thought occurred to me that this is not the way to achieve enlightenment. There is not enough strength in the body to absorb the experience or even to achieve it. So it was then that I ate my first meal."

There was a lovely little girl around who was the daughter of a cattleherder, and she took the milk of a thousand cows and fed it to a hundred, that of a hundred she fed to ten, and the milk of those ten cows she fed to one. There was such power in that concentrated milk that, when she gave the bowl to the Buddha and he drank of it, his whole body was refreshed. When he was finished, he threw the bowl into the river and said, "If this bowl goes upstream, I shall become a Buddha." It went upstream. That night the illumination came.

> Fear of your power
> is what commits you
> to the lower system.

If in me there is the kind of power that can stand against the tide of history, then I can become disengaged from it. Nietzsche says, "Beware of spitting against the wind." You know what will happen. But if you can spit against the wind and it hits somebody else in the eye, then you're going to be a Buddha.

I've always looked for signs like that. When I had to register for the drafts, behind the desks there were three men and one woman. I said if the woman calls me, I won't be drafted. The woman called me, and just when it was time for me to be taken in, they learned

211

that I was thirty-eight, and they could not use people of that antiquity. I think, as do the Buddhists, that what is to be is somehow implicit in what is, and that to look for such signs is a natural and amusing thing to do.

In our tradition, we do not operate in accordance with those fixed patterns. We believe that the ego, which makes value judgments and decisions for action, brings about change. Freud speaks of the ego as "the reality principle," that which puts you in touch with "reality," reality with a small "r": meaning, the individual circumstances of your life and your relationship to those circumstances. And in our culture, the ego, the evaluating principle, is developed. The mother asks, "What kind of ice cream do you want, Johnny, strawberry or vanilla?" "I want vanilla." And he gets vanilla.

In the East, by contrast, where everything you do is what you are told to do, they put something in front of you and you get what you are given. And if everything you do is what you are told to do, your ego is not being developed. Consequently, in the East, people have no concept of the ego. They don't know what the ego is. It doesn't play any role. There is no individual evaluation.

In Freudian psychology, the pleasure principle, the "id," the zeal of life for holding on to food, comfort, sex, and life itself—the context I call "health, wealth, and progeny"—is what most people live for. Against the id, Freud posits the "superego," the social laws that discipline the individual, so that one does, not what one wants, but what society says one should do. In the East, in psychological terms, the whole conflict is between superego and id. No ego principle is even considered.

So, without anything that we would call an ego, the Easterner seeking illumination leaves his family, goes to a guru, and brings a little ball or shell, his ego, and he asks the guru to break it. And the guru takes a little mallet, the yoga discipline, and—"bing!"—his ego is gone. But the Westerner going to a guru brings with him a rock-solid ego that's been the guiding force of his whole life. And when he asks the guru to break his ego, the guru takes the same little mallet and goes "bing! bing! bing!" for forty years and nothing happens. The person just feels increasingly unhappy.

I submit that if you are a person with an evaluating psyche. who is having thoughts no guru ever had, there must be another way to have illumination. I think what Ramakrishna calls "the monkey way" can, in our culture, turn into the equivalent of the Buddhist "middle way." That is to say, when you have found the center within yourself that is the counterpart of the sacred space, you do not have to go into the forest. You can have a technique for extracting your own repose from that center. You can live from that center, even while you remain in relation to the world.

There is a popular Indian fable that Rama-krishna used to like to tell, to illustrate the difficulty of holding in mind the two conscious planes simultaneously, of the multiple and transcendent. It is of a young aspirant whose guru had just brought home to him the realization of himself as identical in essence with the power that supports the universe and which in theological thinking we personify as "God." The youth, profoundly moved, exalted in the notion of himself as at one with the Lord and Being of the Universe, walked away in a state of profound absorption; and when he had passed in that state through the village and out onto the road beyond it, he beheld, coming in his direction, a great elephant bearing a howdah on its back and with the mahout, the driver, riding—as they do—high on its neck, above its head. And the young candidate for sainthood, meditating on the proposition "I am God; all things are God," on perceiving that mighty elephant coming toward him, added the obvious corollary, "The elephant also is God." The animal, with its bells jingling to the majestic rhythm of its stately approach, was steadily coming on, and the mahout above its head began shouting, "Clear the way! Clear the way, you idiot! The youth, in his rapture, was thinking still, "I am God; that elephant is God." And, hearing the shouts of the mahout, he added, "Should God be afraid of God? Should God get out of the way of God?" The phenomenon came steadily on with driver at its head still shouting at him, and the youth, in undistracted meditation, held both to his place on the road and to his transcendental insight, until the moment of truth arrived and the elephant, simply wrapping its great trunk around the lunatic, tossed him aside, off the road.

Physically shocked, spiritually stunned, the youth landed all in a heap, not greatly bruised but altogether undone; and rising, not even adjusting his clothes, he returned, disordered, to his guru, to require an explanation. "You told me," he said, when he had explained himself, "you told me that I was God." "Yes," said the guru, "you are God." "You told me that all things are God." "Yes," said the guru again, "all things are God." "That elephant, then, was God?" "So it was. That elephant was God. But why didn't you listen to the voice of God, shouting from the elephant's head, to get out of the way?"[112]

> Wisdom and foolishness
> are practically the same.
> Both are indifferent
> to the opinions of the world.

According to legend, when Avalokiteshvara looked down upon this suffering world he was filled with such compassion that his head burst into innumerable heads...while from his body sprang a thousand helping arms and hands, like an aura of dazzling rays, and in the palm of each hand there appeared an eye of unimpeded vision....

Every pore of the body of Avalokiteshvara contains and pours forth thousands of Buddhas, saints of all kinds, entire worlds. From his fingers flow rivers of ambrosia that cool the hells and feed the hungry ghosts....He appears to brahmans as a brahman, to merchants as a merchant, to insects as an insect, to each in the aspect of its kind....[113]

"*T*HE *goddess alone knew of the all-moving, secret world energy which had helped the gods to victory; it was the power within them, of which they were unaware. They believed that they were strong in themselves, but without this force, or against it, they could not so much as harm a blade of grass. The goddess knew of the universal force, which the Vedic priests called* brahman *and which Hindus call* sakti, *for* sakti, *i.e. energy, is the essence and name of the Great Goddess herself, hence she could explain the mysterious being to the gods, she could teach them its secret—for it was her own secret.*"—Zimmer[114]

In Hinduism, all power, *sakti*, is female. So, the female represents the totality of the power, and the male is imaged as the agent of the female. In that sense, the power that a female feels from the male—the animus, in Jungian terms—is a specification of the female power, a mode of application of that power.

Every being has a twofold aspect, reveals a friendly and a menacing face. All gods have a charming and a hideous form, according to how one approaches them; but the Great Goddess is the energy of the world, taking form in all things. All friendly and menacing faces are facets of her essence. What seems a duality in the individual god, is an infinite multiplicity in her total being....

She is the mute security of life in itself; from the ashes of burned forests she raises eager fresh flowers whose decay is pregnant with new life, a new life which all around it sees only life in its transitions and transformations with no shadow of death, just as we ourselves, when we sink our teeth into a ripe fruit, or draw a living plant from the garden, are without awareness of death.

Whatever you do, in waking or sleeping, consciously or involuntarily in the cycle of your flesh to the accompanying music of your soul; whatever you do as your body builds and destroys, absorbs and excretes, breathes and procreates, or bestows joy infringing on the limits of rage and pain—all this is a mere gesture of the Great Mother, jaganmayi (consisting of all worlds and beings), who unremittingly does likewise with her world body in endless thousands of forms.... To see the twofold, embracing and devouring, nature of the goddess, to see repose in catastrophe, security in decay, is to know her and to be saved....She is the perfect figuration of life's joyous lures and pitiless destruction: the two poles charged with the extremest tension, yet forever merging.—Zimmer[115]

Also, in Hinduism, the sun is female and the moon is male: he is born of her, dies into her, and is born of her again every month. Shiva, this great power, is the moon god. Parvati, his consort, is the sun power. And although the worship in the masculine-oriented action systems in India is directly to Shiva, it's to the goddess Kali, that the worship finally goes. So that, actually, in India, Kali is the great divinity.

...the Hindu goddess Kali...is shown standing on the prostrate form of the god Shiva, her spouse. She brandishes the sword of death, i.e., spiritual discipline. The blood-dripping human head tells the devotee that "he that loseth his life for her sake shall find it." The gestures of "fear not" and

"bestowing boons" teach that she protects her children, that the pairs of opposites of the universal agony are not what they seem, and that for one centered in eternity the phantasmagoria of temporal "goods" and "evils" is but a reflex of the mind— as the goddess herself, though apparently trampling down the god, is actually his blissful dream.[116]

> The Goddess
> gives birth to forms
> and kills forms.

It's interesting that in the North, in the European systems—and in the Chinese system, where one hears of *yang and yin*—the man is the aggressor, the active principle, and the woman is the receptive and passive aspect. It's just the opposite in India. The Hindu position is that woman is the *śakti*, the serpent power that comes up the spine, the life-energy principle. She's the activator, and the man just wants to be left alone. The man, psychologically, is interested in other things, but when this power field goes by, he's activated. As Joyce writes in *Finnegans Wake*, "With lipth she lithpeth to him all to time of thuch on thuch and thow and thow. She he she ho she ha to la."[117] And wouldn't it be nice to sthart the world again? And he thinks, "My god, yeah, it would." And that's it, he's gone. He gets involved that way because she's the whole damned energy in any of it's aspects.

Similarly, in the mythological systems of what we call, basically, the Bronze Age, the female was the great divinity and the source of all power. For instance, in the Egyptian image of the Pharaoh on the throne, the throne being what gives him his authority, the throne is the goddess Isis. The same mythic image comes up in Byzantine iconography of the Virgin and the Christ: the Christ Child sits on the Virgin's knee just the way the Pharaoh sits on the throne: she is his power. He is called the world ruler, but she's behind him all the way. Likewise, in old pictures of Presidents of the United States, one usually sees the President's wife standing behind him. She's Isis, and he's the child on the throne.

There is a Pygmy dance where the woman ties the whole male community up with a rope. They stand there completely immobilized and one of them says, "She has made us all silent." Then she loosens them, and as each one is loose, he sings. They know this basic, basic mythological stuff that we've lost.

Her womb is the field of space, her heart the pulse of time, her life the cosmic dream of which each of our own lives is a reflex; and her charm is the attractive power, not of a yonder *shore, but of* this. *In short: in Biblical terms, she is Eve; or rather, Eve extended to be the mother, not only of mankind but of all things, the rocks and trees, beasts, birds and fish, the sun and moon and stars.*[118]

The male power comes in with the Semites and Indo-European Aryans, masculine-oriented societies of herding peoples for whom the specific function of the energy was to control the animals on the plains. Then you have the problem of the relationship between male and female mythologies.

> Where agriculture
> is a main means of support,
> there are earth and goddess powers.

> Where hunting predominates,
> it's male initiative
> that empowers the killing of animals.

In the Semitic tradition, the goddess is wiped out, and a prominent feature of that orthodoxy is a masculine fear of the female body, the prime anthropomorphic symbol of Nature's allure and power. This went to such extremes in Christianity that nuns were not even allowed to look at their bodies. In Islam, the most male-oriented of the modern religions, a woman is nothing but a vehicle for producing sons, and the male function is, in large part, the protection of the women. I was in Pakistan for only a few hours, but what I saw!

Those women were going around in tents! Even their eyes were covered with cheesecloth, so you did not know if it was an old hag or a glorious goddess walking around. And you can't respond to a tent.

> Male = social order.
> Female = nature order.

> The male's job is to relate to life.
> The female's job is to become it.

The prime function of the male is to set up an ecological situation in which the woman can give birth, to prepare the field so that the female may bring forth the future, because she is the life. She is the totality. He is a protecting factor, the agent of her power. If a woman loses her husband, she has to take over a male role, but it is a mistake to regard that as something foreign to her own energy. The animus function is in every woman, but it is usually delegated to somebody.

What I think has happened now—with so many women, left without husbands, being thrown into the field of male achievement—is that women have been sold a bill of goods—perhaps not intentionally, but actually. With our strong emphasis on such dramatic and conspicuous male activities as building cities filled with skyscrapers and sending jet-propelled rockets to the moon, women have come to believe that only the aims and virtues of the male are to be considered, and that male achievement is the proper aim for everyone, as though that is what counts. No indeed.

Women used to know how to run the world, but when they move into the secondary energy position of doing the job of the man—who is, in fact, just the agent of the female power—women lose their real power and become resentful. Spengler said, in a telling sentence that got into me when I read it: "Man makes history. Woman is history." She's what it is about, and the man fashions the field within which she can produce history and be history.

> The man's function is to act.
> The woman's function is to be.
> She's "It." She is Mother Earth.

So, the female is "It." When you say the woman brings forth children, that's part of just *being*, fulfilling a role that is already there in the very body itself. And the production need not be children. It can be in representing that power, that quality, that being in life which the woman represents. This is why the woman's beauty or quality of character is so important in mythological tales, which does not mean that a woman who's not physically beautiful does not have this power. It's right there in the female presence.

The mythological figure of the Universal Mother imputes to the cosmos the feminine attributes of the first, nourishing and protecting presence. The fantasy is primarily spontaneous; for there exists a close and obvious correspondence between the attitude of the young child toward its mother and that of the adult toward the surrounding material world. [119]

When Heinrich Zimmer, a great devotee of the Goddess, was trying to find his place in America, he was helped by the old ladies of the Jung Foundation. They were getting him jobs, helping his wife to find a place and so forth. He said, "When I look into those eyes, I say, 'I see you there.'" So, she's operative in every woman in a way that the god is not operative in a man. I'll never forget that wonderful twinkle in his eye when he said, "I see you there."

Woman, in the picture language of mythology, represents the totality of what can be known. The hero is the one who comes to know. As he progresses in the slow initiation which is life, the form of the goddess undergoes for him a series of transfigurations: she can never be greater than himself, though she can always promise more than he is yet capable of comprehending. She lures, she guides, she bids him burst his fetters. And if he can match her import, the two, the knower and the known, will be released from every limitation. Woman is the guide to the sublime acme of sensuous adventure. By deficient eyes she is reduced to inferior states; by the evil eye of ignorance she is spellbound to banality and ugliness. But she is redeemed by the eyes of understanding. The hero who can take her as she is, without undue commotion but with the kindness and assurance she requires, is potentially the king, the incarnate god, of her created world. [120]

A little girl has a golden ball. Now gold is the incorruptible metal, the sphere is the perfect sphere, and the circle is her soul. She likes to go out to the edge of the forest, the abyss, and sit beside a little pool, a little spring, the entrance to the underworld, and there she likes to toss her soul around: toss the little ball and catch it, toss the ball and catch it, toss the ball and—bing!—she misses it, and it goes down into the pond.

She starts to weep. She has lost her soul. This is depression. This is loss of energy and joy in life. Something has slipped out. It is the counterpart of Helen of Troy being stolen in the classic story of the *Iliad:* Helen of Troy was stolen, so they want to get her back.

So, the little golden ball has dropped, her soul has been swallowed by the wolf of the underworld. Now, when the energy goes down like that, the power that's at the bottom of the pool, the inhabitant of the under-world, comes up—a dragon, or in this case, a little frog. He says "What's the matter, Little Girl?" And she tells him, "I've lost my golden ball." And he says, "I'll get it for you." And she says, "That would be very nice." And he says, "What will you give me?"

Now, she has to give up something, there has to be some kind of exchange, so she says, "I will give you my golden crown." He says, "I do not want your golden crown." "I'll give you my pretty silk dress." "I don't want your pretty silk dress." "Well," she demands, "what do you want?" "I want to eat with you at the table, be with you as your playmate, sleep with you in your bed." So, underestimating the frog, she says, "Okay, I'll do that."

The frog dives down and brings up the ball. Now he is the hero who is on the adventure. She, without so much as a thank you, takes the ball and goes trotting home, and he comes flopping after her, saying, "Wait for me." He's very slow.

She gets home, and that evening, when the little princess and King Daddy and Queen Mother are having dinner, doing very nicely with their meal, this green creature comes flopping up the front steps: plomp, plomp, plomp. The girl goes a bit pale, and her father asks, "So, what's the matter? What's that?" And she says, "Oh, just a little frog I met." And he says, "Did you make any promises?"

Now there's the moral principle coming in; you have to correlate all these things. So, when she answers, "Yes," the king says, "Well, then, open the door and let him in." So, in comes the frog, and he's down on the floor, and then he says, "I want to be on the table. I want to eat off of your golden plate." Well, that spoils dinner. The dinner is finished, and she goes up to bed. He comes flopping up the stairs after her and bangs against the door, saying, "I want to come in." So she opens the door and lets him in. "I want to sleep in your bed with you." Well, that is more than she can take.

There are several ways of ending this part of the story, but the one I like best is where she just picks up the frog and throws him against the wall. The frog cracks open, and out steps this beautiful prince, with eyelashes like a camel. It seems he had also been in trouble: he had been cursed by a hag into the condition of a frog. Now that's the little boy who hasn't dared to move on into adulthood. She is the little girl who is at the brink of adulthood. Both of them are refusing it, but each now helps the other out of this dilemma, and it's a beautiful, beautiful experience.

Then, the story says, the next morning, after they had been married, a coach comes to the front door. It was his coach. He was a prince, after all, whose kingdom had been in desolation since his transformation into a frog. So he and his bride get into the coach, and as they are driving away, they hear a loud sound: Bang! He says to the coachman, "What's the matter, Henry? What's happened?" And Henry says, "Well, ever since you have been gone, my Prince, there have been four bands of iron around my heart. *One* of them has now broken." As they ride further, there are three more "Bangs," and then the heart of the coachman beats properly once again.

The coachman is symbolic of the land that requires the prince as its generating and governing power. He'd failed in his duty and gone down into the underworld, but down in the underworld, he found his little bride.

I like that story particularly, because both of them are in trouble, both are at the bottom of the pond, and each rescues the other in this funny way. Meanwhile, the world up there has been waiting for its prince to return. So that is one example of the hero journey.

THE question that comes—always, always, always—is: "What about the woman's journey?" The woman's life, if she is following the biologically grounded norm, is that of life in the world, in one relationship or another to a family. Then when the retirement time comes, the normal passage is into the stage which can be pictured as the Grandmother, of giving advice to the new life coming along. One can be in a position of being a grandmother to the grandchildren of the world. One is in a role, then, of mature, life-fostering advice. The woman brings forth life in one way or another, either biologically or socially, and then, in the latter stage, is life-fostering and life-guiding. The man is more inward than the woman in that last stage.

The relationship of age to childhood, it seems to me, is a very sweet thing. There is a sweet, amusing picture of Ida Rolf and a little child looking at each other, west to east, across the distance of life: the whole, historically conditioned stage between is missing, and there's just one eternity looking at the other. If you can be in some kind of social relationship that enables that principle of the eternal experience to look at the eternal innocence and foster it, that is really archetypal.

In cases throughout history, however, where there have been inadequate responses to what the woman is doing—that is to say, she is doing what nature and society expect, but it's an arid and bad situation—this is what I would term a "call to adventure." And if a woman engages in the man's task of entering the field of achievement, then her mythology will be essentially the same as that of the male hero.

The heroine will, of course, encounter difficulties and advantages which are not those that the male meets, but whether one is male or female, the stages of the inner journey, the visionary quest, are the same, even though the imagery is going to be a little different. For instance, the central image in a man's mandala is often some radiant jewel, or gem, or something like that, but the central image for a woman might be of her holding a child in her arms, the child of her spiritual birth, since the imagery of biological commitment is translated even to the spiritual forms.

My wife, who is anything but the housewife, has no trouble in seeing the male hero as the counterpart of the female hero, if the woman is engaged in the kind of task that has traditionally been seen as a male task; that is to say, if she is engaged in achieving something, rather than waiting in solitude to be achieved, which is the woman's normal role. Jean is an artist, richly fulfilled in an active role, and her crises are essentially the same as a male's crises. The women we know with whom she has worked are also not typical housewives. They have a-chieved fulfillment in the realm of the arts, which is the only place I know of—except, perhaps, for academe—where women can have this unconventional way of life. In my own work, I have known a lot of women in the world of "the head trip," but they never seemed to me to be as richly fulfilled as the ones that went into the arts. Their fulfillment was more in the way of achieve-ment, whereas the artists' fulfillment was in doing what the artist does, and that is a different thing.

In all of literature there is very little of the woman's adventure because she is already "It," and her problem is the realization of that. There are quite a few adventures of little girls in *Grimm's Fairy Tales*, and most of them have to do with the hesitation before moving into the threshold of accepting womanhood.: the sleeping princess, and all that sort of thing, and then the waking. When women dream, often their active aspect appears in male form.

What the male represents is the agent of the feminine power directed to a specific kind of functioning. In the male body, however, there's not the recall to female nature that there is automatically in the female body. Consequently, a male going forth and finding the place of, the instrument of, his full power would not have the problem of discovering the feminine factor in himself, for it is quite slight compared with the feminine factor in the female body. It is a greater distance from what the body has given you. It's a matter of proportion.

> A man must do.
> He must disengage from the mother
> and find his way of "doing,"
> which is a way of pain.
> A woman has only to be.

In my twenties, I lived with artists, many of them women. I noticed that when they approached the age of thirty, the marriage problem came up with each one. "I have to get married now and have a child." When the female within calls the sculptor who has found her instruments of power, the mallet and chisel, her art falls apart because she can't carry a serious art career unless she is at it, and nothing else, all day long.

228

This wreckage doesn't happen with men. When the female calls the male, all he does is go and get married, because the female is out there, where she naturally is. I would say that this is one of the points in the female journey: there is a heavier load of given nature to deal with. It starts with the girl being overtaken by the menstrual moment, and then she's a woman.

That much of a summons to life is the problem that you ladies have that we men don't. Your whole body tells you that you have disowned it. A man does not have that problem. A woman can follow the hero's journey, but there will be other calls and another relationship that's asked of her, namely, to the nature field of which she is the manifestation.

It took me a long time to get around to marriage, principally because I felt that women always wanted to have fun, and that was not my interest at all. It would interfere with my reading. That's really the truth. But another reason was that every time I would get really involved with a woman, I'd have the feeling of weight: life was heavy. And pretty soon I'd just get fed up with that heaviness, with that feeling of everything being so goddamn important and all these little bits of things becoming mountainous problems, and—Jesus!: "I'm out." And then, a little while later, here it is again.

I have taught hundreds of young women, many of whom have gone into the arts, as did Jean, who went into classic dance. But many of the others had husbands who would not stand for that. Each of these woman had to make a choice, and if she chose to knuckle down to what her husband wanted, that ended her adventure. It really did. Everything else then became a substitute. But the objective is to have your own adventure, not a substitute, and it is not by any means an easy thing to do.

When I was teaching these young women, I wasn't thinking of turning them into philologists or historians. So what was I giving them this stuff for? Most were going to get married, have children, and give themselves to daily chores—comparable to my daily chore of teaching them, which, after the first excitement, was no fun either. But there are many ways of using the material, and my thought was this: they will have their families, and then, when they are fifty and their families have been launched, there they'll be. And it was my intention to give them this spiritual message of how to read the world in the second half of life's journey. That was a long time ago. I still know many of these women —twenty, thirty, or forty years later—and I hear unanimously, that my approach worked, that I gave them something that is now feeding this aspect of their lives.

It's interesting that in traditions like the Japanese or the old Oriental, and this goes all the way back to Greece in Plato's time, the housewife was one kind of woman, and the courtesan was another. The courtesan was the woman proficient in the arts, in literature, and in talk. It was a different type of human life from that of the housewife, and in those traditions, the woman was fulfilled in that role.

Then there's another woman's role in literature, but one I have never seen, that of the woman who appears as an Amazon. There is one such story about the daughter of the King of France, who's been kidnapped by the Muslims. After she and a Muslim fall infinitely in love, she is rescued by her family and brought back from Islam. Her Muslim lover follows, recaptures her, and now, as they are running to escape from this military group of brothers who are trying to take her back, she says to him, "How good are you with your sword?" He says, "No good. I'm just good in bed." "Well," she replies, "you go on then, and I will take care of this bunch." It is a wonderful story, one of the best in the world, and it's worth looking for in the *Arabian Nights*.

Joyce speaks of the woman as the one who is the link between: between nations, between people. The ability women have to marry men of totally alien cultures and find themselves at home with them is more than what happens when men marry women of alien cultures. Woman is the link between. Another thing that Joyce brings out in *Finnegans Wake*: a woman has three or four sons: one is a great son, another is a poor son. She loves them all. She is not evaluating in terms of achievements or anything of the kind. She represents a human-to-human relationship.

> Where male power dominates,
> you have separation.
> Where female power dominates,
> there's a non-dual, embracing quality.

Having taught young women, I've been amazed to see how competent they are in understanding their husband's job, if they are in a marriage that's really going. She never studied that stuff, but she's right in there with him, because any failure on the part of either member

ruins the duad. In my own case, everything that I write
I read to Jean, who gives me the criticism and support
that my work requires. The man might feel sometimes
as though he does not need cooperation, but he does.
There is a big difference between a man operating with
a woman behind him and one out there alone.

When we were first married, and I was driving the
car, it didn't matter what the hell I did, Jean went along
with it. Then there came a time when I realized there
would have been a psychological transformation, that
some-times she was critical of the way my driving was
done. There then came a stage where she was directing,
And all of that was acceptable: it had to do with
changes in her thinking. First, she thought, "Anything
he does is great." Then, when she had learned a little
more about me, her uncritical acceptance went away.
Finally, after she had learned still more about me—and
it always goes like this—now, she is the boss. I know
the feeling of turning a car over to someone and just
having to say, "If we run into something, that's okay.
Here we go, Dear." And you find that she manages
very well. It's different, that's all. It is the Perilous Bed.

> A knight, in full armor,
> approaches the Perilous Bed.
> Whenever he tries to settle into it,
> the bed jumps and bucks and moves.
>
> The Perilous Bed represents
> the female temperament.
>
> If the male can just hold on,
> if he can endure,
> the bed will settle down,
> and he'll get the reward.

Some time ago, I had a sabbatical and spent the whole year traveling, mostly in India and Japan, but I was also in Thailand, Ceylon, Burma, and Taiwan. My impression was that, in anything, the women in these cultures were more competent than the men. Perhaps I had to go abroad to see something that is also a fact back here, but I was tremendously impressed by the vigor and authority of Oriental women.

I was a long time in India, and since I had already published the Zimmer books, I saw every department of India that one could ask to see, including the house of Nehru. His younger sister took me as her person-to-go-to-parties-with, so I met the whole bunch. Indian women look so darned humble with their saris and all, but they are nothing of the kind. They are potent. In Japan, however, it is a different situation, because those men are really strong men. But when you see a Japanese couple in a restaurant, who pays the check? The woman. She has the money.

The principle characterization of Athene is as the guardian of heroes, as a patroness, like Laksmi, the Indian goddess who is the supporter of the king or of anybody who then becomes her hero. We find Athene depicted in art as the protector of heroes: she is there when Perseus takes the head of Medusa, and she is the one who initiates the young man into his heroic career. In the *Odyssey,* she tells Telemachus to go find his father. She is present when Odysseus lands on the island of Scherie and meets the Phaeacian princess Nausicaa, and she is again present at the meeting of father and son. So, we can think of her as the guardian of heroes.

Athene is also the protectress of the Acropolis, the fortress of the city. Athene relates to the father, not to the mother. Her mother was Metis, but when Metis was pregnant, Zeus swallowed her, so she gave birth to her child in Zeus' belly, and Athene emerged from his head. That's what Freud calls a transfer to above—the birthplace of the male creation—and she comes forth from there. In societies with such traditions, as I see it, the mother is the mother of our nature. The child is born of the mother and is the little nature object. The father is the parent of one's social maturity. Hence, in the boy's initiation, he goes from the mother to the men's camp, and they initiate him.

> Father is the separator.
> Mother brings together.

Hera is the consort of Zeus, who represents royal rule, the justice that governs the world, so she is matron of the household. This role is different from that of Athene, patron of the heroic adventure. In the contrast between seductress and wife, Hera is the wife, and the seductress role goes to Aphrodite. Aphrodite, however, is more than just the seductress. She is the goddess of all love, a tremendously powerful figure, for love can overtake a person as seductress, but it is also the supporting love of life.

The Ouranian Venus is the one who gives the inspiration of the muses that is the inspiration of the spirit. She feeds not only the body but the spirit as well. The way she pours life into the world shows that this one life is the one truth of all things. That's why I think that the woman as artist is in a field which furnishes not only physical life but spiritual life as well—the spiritual life at once the revealing power.

I have noticed that the way women look at children is different from the way men do. There are two ways of looking at a little kid in an airplane toddling up and down the aisle: one is the way the woman looks at the child; the other is the way the man does. That's why I say that the prime female power and virtue is compassion: the lack of egoistic isolation , the opening to participation. Even in sex, the man is aggressive, but the woman opens. The opening to that ubiquitous presence which is the ground of us all is compassion. Recognizing that spontaneous feeling, embracing it, and manifesting it in action is the female power.

In my book *The Mythic Image.*, I have a wonderful story about Kuan-yin, one of the personifications of the great Mahāyāna Bodhisattva Avalokiteshvara, the embodiment of compassion.[121]

It seems that Kuan-yin realized that in a certain part of China, out in the rural areas, nobody had ever heard of enlightenment. They were all interested in horse racing and all this macho stuff. So she turns herself into a gloriously beautiful girl, comes into town with fresh fish from the river to sell, and when her basket is empty, she disappears. Early the next day, this beautiful fish-selling girl is there again, and then once again she disappears. This daily pattern continues, and soon all of the men have become enchanted by her.

One morning, when she appears, about ten or twenty of them surround her and say, "You have to marry one of us." "Well," she says, "I cannot marry twenty men, but tommorrow morning, if one of you can recite by heart the Sutra of the Compassionate Kuan-yin, I will marry that man." The next morning, a dozen men know the entire sutra by heart, so she says, "Well, I cannot marry all of you, but I will marry the one who can interpret this sutra to me tomorrow."

The next day, there are four men who can interpret the sutra, so now she says, "I am only one woman, and I can't marry four men, but if one of you has *experienced* the meaning of this sutra three days from now, then I will marry that man."

Three days later, there is but one man waiting for her. Now she says, "My little house is down by the bend in the river. Come there this evening, and you will be my husband."

So that evening, he goes to where the shore bends and comes to a little house. An old couple is standing

236

outside, and the old man says, "Oh, we've been waiting a long, long time for you. Our daughter is inside." But when he goes into the room, it's empty. She isn't there. So he looks out the window and sees footprints, which he follows down to the river, where he finds a little pair shoes at the water's edge, but no girl.

Then, as he's standing there, with the reeds blowing and so forth, he realizes that all the reeds and everything else is she. Through her allure and charm, which is what the female figures represent in these Mahāyāna images, he realizes the nirvāṇic grace of beauty in the universe. Having understood the sutra, he knew what he was experiencing, and he received illumination.

Dante realized something of this kind at the end of *The Divine Comedy.* He had followed the allure of Beatrice, who had guided him through the heavens to the very throne of God, and when he got there, she was there, together with the Trinity and the angelic forms. Behind the three persons of the Trinity, he saw three circles of flame and light, which represented the nonpersonal aspect of the god. He said that he was wondering how the personified forms and non-personified illumination could be the same, when suddenly he understood that the whole world was of the love and grace of God: the love he'd first experienced in Beatrice.

> When it's all love,
> all must be love.
> Nothing must interfere:
> love conquers all.

Living
in the Sacred

*N*OW the Indian term for "illusion," māyā—*from the verbal root* mā, *"to measure, to measure out, to form, to create, construct, exhibit or display"—refers to both the power that creates an illusion and the false display itself. The art of a magician, for example, is māyā; so too the illusion he creates. The arts of the military strategist, the merchant, actor, and thief: these also are māyā. Māyā is experienced as fascination, charm; specifically, feminine charm. And to this point there is a Buddhist saying: "Of all the forms of māyā that of woman is supreme."* [122]

Let's say we have the world of that which is no world: the Garden of Eden *before* the world of duality, the transcendent mystery. Then we have the world of things: the world of duality and multiplicity, of māyā, where we've lost connection with the transcendence.

> Maya is that power
> which converts transcendence
> into the world.

As a cosmogenic principle—and as a feminine, personal principle, also—māyā is said to possess three powers:
1. A Veiling Power that hides or conceals the "real," the inward essential character of things; so that, as we read in a sacred Sanskrit text: "Though it is hidden in all things, the Self shines not forth." [123]

The first stage, the veil, manifests from the fact that you don't see the white light. This is what is called the Maya veil. The image that's given is of white light broken into the colors of the rainbow by a prism. This prism is the Goddess. With the veiling power, the obscuring power, the white light can't get through.

2. A Projecting Power, which then sends forth illusionary impressions and ideas, together with associated desires and aversions—as might happen, for example if at night one should mistake a rope for a snake and experience fright. Ignorance (the Veiling Power), having concealed the real, imagination (the Projecting Power) evolves phenomena. And so we read: "This power of projection creates all appearances, whether of gods or of the cosmos."[124]

With the projecting power, the forms of the world come through. The prism is the veil, but it is also the projector: what stops the white light and what projects the colors of the rainbow. In this second stage, the white light shows through the forms of the world. If you put a number of colors on a disk and spin it, you'll get a *white* spinning disk—that's the revealing power.

These first two powers, concealing and projecting, can be compared to those properties of a prism by which sunlight is transformed into the colors of the rainbow. Arrange these seven colors on a disk, spin it, and they will be seen as white. So too, when viewed a certain way, the phenomena themselves may reveal what normally they veil; which demonstrates:

3. The Revealing Power of māyā, which it is the function of art and scripture, ritual and meditation, to make known.[125]

It is the function of art to serve
the revealing power of māyā.

The old voice of the ocean, the bird-chatter of little rivers,
(Winter has given them gold for silver
To stain their water and bladed green for brown to line
*   their banks)*
From different throats intone one language.
So I believe if we were strong enough to listen without
Divisions of desire and terror
To the storm of the sick nations, the rage of the hunger-
*   smitten cities,*
Those voices also would be found
Clean as a child's; or like some girl's breathing who
*   dances alone*
By the ocean-shore, dreaming of lovers.
                              —Robinson Jeffers[126]

Fear and desire
are the problem of the artist also.

We need more poetry that reveals
what the heart is ready to recognize.

...the first function of art is exactly that which I have
already named as the first function of mythology; to transport
the mind in experience past the guardians—desire and fear—
of the paradisal gate to the tree within of illuminated life. In
the words of the poet Blake, in The Marriage of Heaven
and Hell, *"If the doors of perception were cleansed, every-*
thing would appear to man as it is, infinite."[127] *But the*
cleansing of the doors, the wiping away of the guardians,
those cherubim with their flaming sword, is the first effect of
art, where the second, simultaneously, is the rapture of rec-
ognizing in a single hair "a thousand golden lions."[128]

243

"Any object, intensely regarded, may be a gate of access to the incorruptible eon of the gods."[129] That is James Joyce. The statement is quoted in *Ulysses* by Buck Mulligan. The situation is that Leopold Bloom, thinking of his home problem, is looking intently at a red triangle on the label of a bottle of Bass ale. When someone starts to disturb Bloom, Mulligan stops him, saying, "...preserve a druid silence. His soul is far away. It is as painful perhaps to be awakened from a vision as to be born. Any object, intensely regarded, may be a gate of access...," and so on.

Take, for example, a pencil, ashtray, anything, and holding it before you in both hands, regard it for a while. Forgetting its use and name, yet continuing to regard it, ask yourself seriously, "What is it?"...Cut off from use, relieved of nomenclature, its dimension of wonder opens; for the mystery of the being of that thing is identical with the mystery of the being of the universe —and of yourself. [130]

Art is the transforming experience.

The revelation of art is not ethics, nor a judgment, nor even of humanity as one generally thinks of it. Rather, the revelation is a marveling recognition of the radiant Form of forms that shines through all things.

In the simplest terms, I think we might say that when a situation or phenomenon evokes in us a sense of existence (instead of some reference to the possibility of an assurance of meaning) we have had an experience of this kind. The sense of existence evoked may be shallow or profound, more or less intense, according to our capacity or readiness; but even a brief shock (say, for example, when discovering the moon over city roofs or hearing a sharp bird cry at night) can yield an experi-

ence of the order of no-mind: that is to say, the poetical order, the order of art. When this occurs, our own reality-beyond-meaning is awakened (or perhaps better: we are awakened to our own reality-beyond-meaning), and we experience an affect that is neither thought nor feeling but an interior impact. The phenomenon, disengaged from cosmic references, has disengaged ourselves, by that principle, well known to magic, by which like conjures like. In fact, both the magic of art and the art of magic derive from and are addressed to experiences of this order. Hence the power of the meaningless syllables, the mumbo jumbo of magic, and the meaningless verbalizations of metaphysics, lyric poetry, and art interpretation. They function evocatively, not referentially; like the beat of a shaman's drum, not like a formula of Einstein. One moment later, and we have classified the experience and may be having utterable thoughts and describable feelings about it—thoughts and feelings that are in the public domain, and they will be either sentimental or profound, according to our educa-tion. But according to our life, we have had, for an instant, a sense of existence: a moment of unevaluated, unimpeded, lyric life—antecedent to both thought and feeling; such as can never be communicated by means of empirically verifiable propositions, but only suggested by art.[131]

The goal of life is rapture.
Art is the way we experience it.

I will give you what seems to me to be the most clear and certain exposition of basic esthetic theory I know, namely, that of James Joyce in *A Portrait of the Artist as a Young Man* .

Joyce makes a distinction between what he calls "proper art" and "improper art." By "proper art" he means that which really belongs to art. "Improper art," by contrast, is art that's in the service of something that is not art: for instance, art in the service of advertising. Further, referring to the attitude of the observer, Joyce says that proper art is static, and thereby induces esthetic arrest, whereas improper art is kinetic, filled with movement: meaning, it moves you to desire or to fear and loathing.

Art that excites desire for the object as a tangible object he calls pornographic. Art that excites loathing or fear for the object he terms didactic. All sociological art is didactic. Most novels since Zola's time have been the work of didactic pornographers, who are preaching a social doctrine of some kind and fancying it up with pornographic icing.

Say you are leafing through a magazine and see an advertisement for a beautiful refrigerator. There's a girl with lovely refrigerating teeth smiling beside it, and you say, "I'd love to have a refrigerator like that." That ad is pornography. By definition, all advertising art is pornographic art. Or suppose you see a photograph of a dear old lady, and you think, "I'd love to have tea with that dear old soul." That photograph is pornography. Or you go into a ski buff's house, where there's a painting of a mountain slope, and you think, "Oh, to go down that mountain slope…" That painting is pornography: your relationship to it is not purely esthetic:

just perceiving the thing. Most of the art that one sees is either didactic or pornographic.

For help with proper art, Joyce goes to Aquinas. He says, and he uses the Latin words, that the esthetic object renders three moments: *integritas,* "wholeness"; *consonantia,* "harmony"; and *claritas,* "radiance."

Say that you have several objects on a table. Put a frame around any portion of this situation, and what is within that frame is now to be regarded not as an assortment of separate objects but as something else: a single entity, a wholeness: *integritas.*

The late Buckminster Fuller has left with us a definition of this way of seeing and appreciating...:

"In order to be able to understand the great complexity of life and to understand what the universe is doing, the first word to learn is synergy. Synergy is the behavior of whole systems, unpredicted by the behavior of their parts. *The most extraordinary example of it is what we call mass attraction. One great massive sphere and another massive sphere hung by tension members are attracted to one another. We find there is nothing in one sphere in its own right, that predicts that it's going to be attracted to another. You have to have the two. It is, then, synergy which holds our earth together with the moon; and it is synergy which holds our whole universe together....Synergy is to energy as inte-* gration is to differentiation."[132]

The Buddhist doctrine of "dependent origination, or mutual arising" (pratitya samutpada) corresponds to this of Fuller's "synergy." When, on the occasion of the Buddha's silent flower sermon (which is regarded traditionally as the founding sermon of Zen), he simply held out to his congregation a single flower, the only one who understood was his foremost disciple, Mahakashyapa, who quietly smiled at him in recognition.[133] In the symbol, which is almost univer-

sal in the Orient, of the universe as a lotus and the lotus as manifest sign on the surface of the waters of an invisible life below waves, the Buddhist doctrine is already implicit of pratītya samutpāda, *"dependent origination, or mutual arising"; for the petals are not to be interpreted as in any way independent of each other, casual or consequential of each other. The whole system has simply arisen, "thus come"* (tathāgata), *like the Buddha himself.*[134]

Now, when you have *integritas,* wholeness inside such a frame, the only thing that counts is the harmonious placement of everything, the *consonantia* , what Joyce calls the "rhythm of beauty,"[135] which includes the relationship of colors to each other, of masses to each other, and of the spaces in between. All elements are part of this harmonious rhythm. When the rhythm is fortunately achieved, one experiences the *claritas,* or radiance: one sees that the aesthetic object is itself and no other thing, and one is held in esthetic arrest.

"The mind," [Joyce] writes, "is arrested and raised above desire and loathing."[136] *The original, biological function of the eye, to seek out and identify things to eat and to alert the mind to danger, is for a moment, or (in the case of a true artist) for a lifetime suspended, and the world (beheld without judgment of its relevance to the well-being of the observer) is recognized as a revelation sufficient in itself.*[137]

In other words, the frame is a border hermetically sealing-off the object, so that all you are experiencing, all that matters, is within that border. It's a sacred field, and you become pure subject for a pure object. You no longer have to know what these things are named or what can be done with them. This is the a–b–c of esthetics. Next comes the d–e–f.

The mystery of art is why one rhythm fixes you in esthetic arrest and another doesn't. Music is nothing if not rhythm. Rhythm is the instrument of art. Music is the organization, not only of rhythm, but of scale and of the notes played against each other: quarter notes, half notes, and so forth. If you are playing a C-Major chord and move to a dominant Seventh, that's an organization of the relationship of one note to another. It is really space.

It's wonderful to see a jazz group improvise: when five or six musicians are really tuned in to each other, it's all the same rhythm, and they can't go wrong, even though they never did it that way before.

The Pygmy people have little pipes that each sound one note, and a bunch of them sit around, each piping one note, and when they get going, something darling comes out: like birds, like forest noises.

Indian music never has a beginning and never has an end. The music represents a plane of consciousness and is going on all the time. When you go to a concert, it's the strangest event. They're fooling around with the instruments, tuning and zinging them, and this may go on for a half hour. Then presently they're playing. It is as though the music were going on continuously, and the musicians simply dip down, pick it up, play with it for a while, and then leave it. It is altogether different from western music: there is not only no tension or release, but no beginning and no end. It's always there.

There's a relationship between musical organization and architectural organization. All architecture is an organization in space. It happens to have a function that is also related to space. The Century Club in New York was built by Sanford White, an important architect, around the end of the nineteenth century. The building is an historical monument. The lounge floor is very harmonizing: a room so proportioned that it puts you at peace. But why this happens is mysterious.

The only answer I can think of is Cezanne's: "Art is a harmony parallel to nature." There are, of course, two natures involved: Nature, the world out there, and the world of nature within. That is to say, when it is the artist's intention is to arrange "a harmony parallel to nature"—and any other intention probably involves didactics or pornography—then that harmony resonates with something inside you, fixes you in esthetic arrest, and you have that big "a-ha!" experience. So it is the function of art to open the consumable things of the tangible, visible world, so that the radiance—the same radiance that's within you—shines through them.

I think one feels this harmony most powerfully in Japan, where your own nature is constantly invoked, and you don't know where Nature ends and art begins. When a garden is constructed, the man who composes it tells his son when to bend each branch: "When it grows out to here, bend it"—so that it looks like Nature. It is art: Nature that has been harmonized with the nature within. That harmony is the first stage of this rhythm. This is basic. Abstract art, any kind of art, has to be thought of in terms of this rhythm. Choosing what verse form you are going to use in poetry in relation to what it is you are going to say, the echoing of one consonant against another: it is all rhythm, to be conceived of in terms of sensuous rhythmic effects that touch you. Certain rhythms render certain responses.

And the two kinetic movements that block this harmonious rhythm are exactly the two temptations of the Buddha: desire, which draws you to possess the object, and loathing or fear, which turns you away from it. When you move to possess or to turn away from an object, you are reacting to the world of delusory appeals and terrors that maya has projected. And esthetic arrest, the condition of the heart or spirit or whatever not being moved by desire or fear, is precisely the counterpart of the experience of the Buddha under the tree of the immovable spot. It *is* the immovable spot. It is a psychological stasis with respect to your relationships to the forms of the world around you.

The biological urges to enjoy and to master (with their opposites, to loathe and to fear), as well as the social urge to evaluate (as good or evil, true or false), simply drop away, and a rapture in sheer experience supervenes, in which self-loss and elevation are the same. Such an impact is "beyond words;" for it is not such as can be explained by a reference to anything else. The mind is released —for a moment, for a day, or perhaps forever—from those anxieties to enjoy, to win, or to be correct which spring from the net of nerves in which men are entangled. Ego dissolved, there is nothing in the net but life —which is everywhere and forever. The Zen masters of China and Japan have called this state the state of "no-mind." The classical Indian terms are moksa, "release," bodhi, "enlightenment," and nirvāna, "transcendence of the winds of passion." Joyce speaks of "the luminous silent stasis of esthetic pleasure,"[138] when the clear radiance of the esthetic image is apprehended by the mind, which has been arrested by its wholeness and fascinated by its harmony. "The mind," he says, "in that mysterious instant Shelley likened beautifully to a fading coal."[139]

So the esthetic vehicle, the instrument of the rhythm of beauty that induces esthetic arrest, is the revealing power of maya.

One application of the artist's craft is in doing something like making a turkey dinner, another is in creating art that is of no use whatsoever except esthetically. When I use the word "art," it has to do with "divinely superfluous beauty" and esthetic arrest. There's no esthetic arrest in eating a turkey. That's life in action, doing what it has to do, namely eating something that's been killed, putting it into your system. It's totally different from esthetic arrest and recognizing the radiance. Are you going to look at the object or eat it? Eating the object is related to desire and loathing.

The distinction between the two has to do with whether it is the projecting power of maya or the revealing power that is present when you look at the object. It's very important to make a clear distinction between the two. If you're concerned with prospering or failing with the object, eating or not eating it, your perspective involves desire and loathing, the temptations of the Buddha, the projecting power of maya.

This bringing together of Joyce's esthetic theory with the maya idea was a wonderful illumination for me. I just woke up this morning and said, "My god, I have finally got it after eighty years." I have known the implications of esthetic arrest, but I'd never linked it up to the maya idea. It is your mental attitude that determines whether you experience the projecting or the revealing power. The world is there in both modes. It is not that the world changes, it's your consciousness.

Esthetic arrest is the result of this change of focus. "The Kingdom of the Father is spread upon the earth and men do not see it." You see it in esthetic arrest. But to develop the inward depth experienced through this change of focus, those who seek to achieve fully the goal of life should set aside a sacred space. The sacred space, when you think of where it appears in traditional cultures, is for initiations and meditations. If you are so fulfilled already that no further initiations are necessary, then you can do without such a space. But, insofar as you've not struck the ultimate depth and are interested in enriching and building the interior, in addition to the external aspects of your life, then you have to have some place, some way, to practice this.

All the world will open up when you've achieved this inner depth, and your play in life will be informed by this radiance. The Grail Castle is in the field that is adventured in the way of experiencing esthetic arrest. The Grail is the sense of total rapture and spiritual fulfillment that comes from your experience of this hermetically sealed field. It is like probing for oil: you put a pipe down, strike oil, and then realize the oil is under everything. But you first have to go down somewhere to find it, and this is the field of this plunge.

I think if you imagine yourself taking the position of esthetic stasis, you'll understand about withdrawing fear and desire for what happens, and about *saṁsāra* being *nirvāṇa*, the still point in the midst of the turning world. That's all there is to it. Then the world becomes a display of things from which you are disengaged, and yet, voluntarily, you can become engaged: "joyous participation in the sorrows of the world." It is very different from being compulsively linked.

The change of consciousness from stasis to kinesis is the Fall in the Garden. The bondages from which the Buddha disengaged—desire, fear, and social duty—are temporal matters. You can engage in them voluntarily, but compulsive engagement is linked to maya. If you have gotten that, you have gotten all I can give you.

Now Ramakrishna, speaking of Brahman and Śakti —or Devi, the Goddess—says that Brahman is the still point, the milky ocean experienced as stillness;

Śakti is the movement, the joy and the pain; and the two together are one. That's the idea of the Yab-Yum. One thing after another was coming together last night in terms of this simple analysis that Joyce has given us.

Then, in Joyce's analysis, we have the emotions of pity and terror. Now, terror is not the same as fear and loathing. It is the realization of both the transcendent operating principle and the effect of the passage of time: the sorrows of the world. It's static, a still terror, not the terror of flight. It is the realization of compassion: identification with the human sufferer: not the poor sufferer, the black sufferer, the Communist or Fascist sufferer, but the *human* sufferer—which eliminates the sociological didactic. You identify with "the suffering servant," you might say, and the terror goes past all movement to the still point of Goethe's "schaudern": the shudder of realization of the mere phenomenality of the world. That's the whole story.

One might add that, in the way of either lust or love, the female enables the male to make the transit: the seductress lures him to the world, and the virgin— the Virgin Birth mother, Mary—introduces him to the transcendent, the Christ principle that transcends individualism. It seems to me that everything falls right into place with this very simple realization.

My life has been one job, one wife, one image: the Grail. This is known as conservatism. There is a wonderful line in the *Portrait*, where Stephen's friend, who's been hearing all this heretical stuff, asks if he intends to become a Protestant. "I said that I had lost the faith," Stephen replies, "but not that I had lost my selfrespect. What kind of liberation would that be to forsake an absurdity which is logical and coherent and to embrace one which is illogical and incoherent?"[140]

Buddhist art before the first century was mostly narrative: the life of the Buddha and similar discursive art, although the Buddha himself was never depicted. However, with the Mahayana realization that *samsara* is *nirvana* and all things are Buddha things, the earliest Buddha images, and other images, began to appear—all presented as revelatory of that realization— and the art object itself became a revelation of Buddha consciousness. It became transparent to the radiance, *claritas,*. which is what we have been talking about.

In Christian art, by contrast, I don't think you have that concept, because in the orthodoxy tangible things are not regarded as being informed by the Christ. It is only in the Thomas Gospel that we read, "Split the stick, there am I. Lift the stone. I am there." And so, in the Christian tradition, one finds only anecdotal art. The Crucifixion is an anecdote of Jesus's suffering on the cross. It's not a revelation. It doesn't induce esthetic arrest. It's didactic. Early Christian art was meant to be didactic, because nobody could read. In the Gothic period, the story of Christ and his apostles and disciples was rendered as when you go to Chartres Cathedral.

I've been there five times. Once I used a guidebook to identify every figure in every window. They are all references to anecdotes of the Christiian tradition, and I could get the whole of the Christian doctrine there. The Rose Window, however, does reveal the radiance. It is magnificent art. Looking at it, one experiences esthetic arest. And the cathedral itself is an art object.

...within the field of a mythology, the symbolic details reflect, indeed, a local material history and environment, yet they are of an order of the mind, and to be interpreted by the faculty of reason as expressions of a spiritual insight....The

idea of a temple (or European cathedral) is what is here announced, an enclosure wherein every feature is metaphorical of a connoted metaphysical intuition, set apart for ritual enactments.

The heart in such an environment is at home, as it were, in its own place: removed from the chaotic spectacle of the world of waking consciousness, at rest and at peace in the recognition of a harmony (which is of one's own nature) informing the whole terrible scene of lives forever consuming lives. And the function, then, of the ritual is to bring one's manner of life into accord with this non-judgmental perspective in the way, not of crude ego-maintenance in a world one never made, but of synergetic participation in a phantasmagoric rapture.[141]

The town of Chartres lives around that cathedral, just as ancient temple cities used to be centered around the temple, which represented the spiritual information the entire city lived by. We have nothing comparable.

I had the most marvelous experience at Chartres. I had been there for several days going through all of this, and the concierge came to me and asked if I'd like to help him ring the noontime bell. Well, you bet. So we went up the north fleche to where there is a great big bell. The bell is down below you, and there is a seesaw–like thing above it with a little railing across. He stood on one side, I stood on the other, and we hung onto the bar between us. He gave a push, this thing started to move, and our hair was blowing, and then, underneath us: "Bong! Bong!" We were on that damned thing four or five minutes. It was tremendous. Then he brought me down and showed me where he lived.

Now, in a cathedral of that kind there is a nave and a crossing. Then there is an apse and a choir screen that runs around it. That choir screen was wide enough for a little room to be in there. He had his bed in that little room in the choir screen and lived there. You could see out between the figures, and right there was the Black Virgin. Oh, I tell you, he had a privileged life in that place. Everything went together: the imagery, the architecture, the rhythm of the day, going up to ring the bells. It was a beautifully coordinated existence.

In the twelfth and thirteenth centuries, there was a body of stories known as the Miracles of the Virgin that included some wonderful little Romances. One of the cutest—years ago it was turned into a miraculous play in New York—was of a nun who was assigned to scrub the chapel floor just when she had a date with her lover. The imaged Virgin comes down, takes the scrub-brush and pail, and says, "Go on out and have your day." She did not play by the rules of the Cardinals.

Art, then, is the Virgin's medium. Art is the vehicle of the revealing power of maya, the vehicle by which we go from the earth to the transcendent. One can always see the Goddess in the world of art.

In the Protestant community, where Mariolatry is abominated, there is no art. Go into any New England chapel and you'll see that it is very pretty, but hymns are the closest things to art that you'll find. I was raised a Catholic and married Jean, daughter of a Protestant minister, so the first Protestant service I went to was with her. We were standing there singing hymns, and I said to her, "You Protestants do not have images, but just look at the images in this hymn: God coming to my little room and all that kind of thing."

One of the most interesting and amusing services I have experienced was in a beautiful church with marvelous stained-glass windows in Grand Rapids, where I gave a sermon entitled "Trick or Treat," for Halloween, the Celtic festival of All Souls. In the middle of the service, the doors opened, and in came all the children of the congregation wearing masks. The big ones led the way, followed by smaller and smaller kids, until, finally, in came these tiny little tots with these absurd masks. The masked children represented the spirits about to be born. Then they all lined up near one of the upright pianos and sang, "I've been working on my costume, all the live long day." It was really a spiritual experience: the children, the choir—just members of the congregation—it was simply sublime.

Then I got up in this pulpit and, my god, I tell you, the pulpit is a weapon. Now there's art for power: just the placement of that thing—where it is in relation to everybody else. Unless you've stood in a pulpit, you don't realize what you have on your side. When you stand there, nobody can hurt you. You are at the prow of a ship, poised to plow right through that sea of faces down below. I did it twice in two years. The first time, I was a little in awe of the pulpit, but the second time, I really knew how to use it.

An artist, to me, is a person who is a competent practitioner of an art. Somebody who just gets up to splash around is not necessarily an artist. One definition of an artist that I heard someone seriously give is: "anybody who, in the telephone book, calls him or herself an artist." I do not go along with that. Even in the practical arts, the principle of perfection in work is a basic expectation.

An artist is someone who has completed an art work, not a person who merely intended to. Whether or not it is saleable either this year or next affects neither its in-trinsic value nor its intrinsic definition as an art work. Van Gogh never sold a thing, but a couple of his works can make a museum. He was in great psychological trouble, but that man was an artist.

The word artist is used in a number of ways, the two principle ones, the two extremes, being: (a) one competent in performance and (b) an artist in the fine arts. You cannot be an artist in the fine arts unless you are competent in performance, but you can be competent in cooking or acrobatics or whatnot. But the experience of esthetic arrest has to do with the fine arts. One doesn't seek esthetic arrest in looking at a good plumbing job. Its *real* function would be missed.

I heard of an amusing experiment when LSD was first around. Four bridge players were given light doses of LSD, with the understanding that they would then play bridge. When the cards had been dealt and picked up, all they did was look at them. There was no playing of the game. It was esthetic arrest, an example of sacred space. The cards were of no use except for esthetic rapture. The object, formerly in certain relevant situations in the life of secular enjoyment, suddenly becomes a thing-in-itself, a final thing.

In action, it makes a difference whether all you are trying to do is to act or whether you are trying to act competently. It helps a great deal to know what the hell you're doing. What are you going to do well? Are you going to be a painter, a Picasso? Is this where your life achievement is? That is a real sacrifice of life.

Whatever choice you make, there is a period of learning and analyzing, when you are not in action, the body is not in performance. Anyone who has taught somebody a skill has seen this stage, where the student is analyzing and trying to do it, but really not in it. Then, finally, the person is able to give expression to what he or she is intending to express.

My first and strongest experience of this was once when Jean came to Esalen with me and was going to give classes in dance. She got this bunch of people who were not interested in technique, but wanted to dance. What they called creative work was going out, opening their arms, and breathing at the ocean. It was not worth being with them even to see what was going on.

There is nothing esthetic about a bunch of ballet people doing their bar exercises. Then they move into dance and are still thinking about the rules, and their work is contrived. But then, finally, the rules melt and natural spontaneity takes over again. There is an old standard saying about the arts: "You need to learn all the rules, and then forget them." That is to say, let them melt back into pure action.

When young people who've not had the schooling I've had decide they're going in for writing, editing, or something like that, I've noticed they don't really have the full equipment. Working on my books, I've hired intelligent young people to help me with the editorial aspects, only to discover they can't read German, they can't read French, they don't know this, they don't know that. It makes me realize what all those years of schooling gave me. The fantastic amount of work that's all under the water. One sees only the tip of the iceberg.

In writing a book, you are moving along on the wave of your inspiration and intuition, and then you come to a difficult passage, an area you have to cover in order to get from here to there, and your momentum stops. That's when you have to bring in the rules.

Also, in athletics, after you practice and practice, there is a lot you can then do spontaneously. But at certain points, you have to act according to rules for moving the body that are not yet spontaneous to you. I think of pole vaulting or the high hurdles: the time that has to be spent just on the technical posture. Or playing golf: how are you going to hold that club? There is no spontaneity when you are thinking all these things. When that is all absorbed, then you have a stronger propulsion than you had before you were forced to break it all up.

I don't think it is proper at all to take the position that C. P. Snow has: namely, that the science—the knowledge, the mathematical side of life—runs in an opposite direction to the life of spontaneous humanistic action. They supplement each other. In literature, for instance, writing sonnets: it takes a lot of practice to make that kind of structure become something that just pours out, but when it does pour out, it is possible to say things that cannot be said without the sonnet form. Form and expression are very close together.

If you are going to act on the basis of what you know, you cannot just hold onto your knowledge. You have to translate it into a movement. This is the whole thing in the arts. The student studies, studies, studies—learning the techniques, the rules, what it is he must strive for—and when he gets used to doing all of that, then he can move.

261

The creative act is
not hanging on, but yielding
to new creative movement.

Think, for instance, of someone studying the piano.
There is nothing worse than having somebody in the
neighborhood studying the piano, practicing their exercises. There's nothing at all beautiful about them. Their
function is to give you facility. Then presently there
comes a point when you have the facility, it happens
automatically, and you do not have to think, "do…
re…me…fa…." Although analysis facilitates competent
action, your spontaneity of action is inhibited when you
are constantly thinking of the rules. This is true for
everything. The one who attempts to be an artist and
has not learned the craft is never going to be an artist.

If you find you are trying,
go back to school.
You're not ready yet.

There is a big difference between art as therapy,
where the person is trying to become human, and art as
art, where the art carries the person past humanity into
new spheres. The difference is that, in therapy, the technique and the art object are of no importance, since all
you are trying to do is turn a person who's off the track
into someone who is on the track. The therapeutic operation in the art is to bring the person back to his own
self, to turn him into a harmonized human being again.
But art comes from harmonized human beings—"Art is
a harmony parallel to nature." And if the person is not
parallel to nature yet, then art is just a therapy to bring
him or her to that point. Therapeutic art is trying to
"catch up," you might say. It is no art for anybody but
the person who's doing it.

Highly stylized dance, like ballet and Indian dance, is a wonderful example of this thing we are talking about: what has to be learned to manipulate the body, all those exercises, eliminates dance for a while. In Hindu dance, the whole body is taken apart: there are certain things the eyes do, certain things the hands do, and so on. Then it is put back together again, and what you get is a transformation of nature in art. It is nothing to look at until you see a dancer who really can do it, and then, my god, another nature comes in on another plane.

> The dance
> is the highest symbol
> of life itself.

In song and dance man expresses himself as a member of a higher community; he has forgotten how to walk and speak and is on the way toward flying, dancing into the air. His very gestures are of enchantment.... He feels himself to be a god, going about in ecstasy, exalted, like the gods beheld in his dreams....He is no longer an artist, he has become a work of art. In a paroxysm of intoxication the creative power of all nature has come to light in him as the highest rapture of the one that is All. Nature, with its true voice undissembled cries out to us: "Be as I am! I, the primordial ever-creating mother amidst the ceaseless flux of appearances, ever impelling into existence, eternally finding in these transformations satisfaction."—Nietzsche[142]

> Art is the set of wings
> to carry you out of
> your own entanglement.

Spengler makes an interesting distinction between what he calls "art as ornament" and "art as imitation." The prime example of art as ornament is architecture, where a structure is timeless once it is achieved: there it sits. The opposite, art as imitation, would be the dance: if you do not see a particular performance, you'll never see that dance again. It is something of a life moment. It's an idea that has meant a lot to me in realizing the different problems of various artists. One of the sad things about a dancer's career is that such great moments are of an essence, and anybody who was not there missed it. For instance, what about Pavlova? If you didn't see that particular performance, it's gone.

I have lived close to the dance world ever since my marriage to Jean. She had the idea of dance being a *part* of her life, so that when dance in the high style was no longer possible, she was able to handle it: always her life, not her art, was the number one thing. Jean has had an elegant career, and she has had a husband who was willing to see it happen. She was taken into Martha Graham's group just when we were married, and that was a marvelous group of wonderful dancers: Merce Cunningham, Erick Hawkins, Jane Dudley, Jean. Believe me, they were all first-rate dancers.

The big shift that the dancer has to make in later years is that the dance is no longer to be thought of as something in the way of a performance or an exhibition, but rather, like a bird singing, just for itself, and only to the distance the body feels it would be lovely to go. Out of that will come a life, because you are in the center of action of your psyche's need and joy, and that will radiate into the rest of what you are doing. The whole world will join the dance.

All we really want to do is dance.

Sacred Dance is for the gods, not for an audience. This is one of the things that comes up when you try to put folk dance on the stage. It's for the joy of the people doing the dance, and it just does not work any other way. The fact that dance was cut out of our religions way back in the late Middle Ages has turned dance into a purely secular thing.

I'm working on the posthumous papers of a young man who went to India to study dance. He was one of Jean's students at New York University's Tisch School of the Arts, and he became so fascinated with Indian dance that he went to India. He was a young Jew, who had been studying to be a rabbi, and his family was in great distress when he went over there, not only to dance, but to study the dance of Shiva, an alien god. Being a religiously oriented person, he was fascinated by the religious implications of the dance: the god is the dancer, and you have to become the god to worship the god, to find that god in yourself. What he recognized was the total difference in implication between dancing for an audience and dancing for the god. When you are alone and in your own place, you are dancing for the god and identifying with it. This whole idea is basic to Tantra: to worship a god, you must become that god. No matter what you call the god or think it is, the god you worship is the one you are capable of becoming.

The power of a deity is that it personifies a power that is in Nature and in your nature. When you find that level, then you are in play. That is the work of art in general, because art really is a worship.

There are two approaches to choosing a profession. One is to study the statistics on the number of jobs that are going to be available in this or that category in the next ten years and base your life on that. That's following the rim of the wheel. The other, is to ask yourself, "What do I want to do?" If you do that, then you are up against your decision. But if you say, "I am going to do what I want to do," and if you stay with it, then something will happen. You may not have a job, but you will have a life, and it will be interesting.

> In the wheel of fortune,
> wisdom points to the center.
> Youth points to the rim.

I have known dozens of artists, and most of them, unless they become commercial artists, live without knowing where their life is going or how it is going to be. You should see what kids in dance go through, and there are no jobs. If you really want to know what it is like in a profession where there are no jobs, go to an actors' school. It is disheartening to see those young people come in full-of-beans and, boy, do they get it.

The normal situation is that, perhaps for years, you work away at your art, your life vocation, your life-fulfilling field of action, and there's no money in it. You have to live, though, so you get a job, which may be a low-degree activity relative to what you are interested in. You could, for instance, teach people the art you are operating in yourself. So, let's say you have a teaching job, and you also have sacred space and time to perform your own work. Your art is what I would call your work. Your employment is your job.

Then, you are doing so well in your job that your employer wants to move you into a higher position. You'll have to give more to the job than before, and you will receive a higher salary, but your new commitments will cut down on your free time. My advice is: don't accept the promotion. Don't accept anything that piles more on you than what you must do to earn your base income, because you are developing, not in your job, but in your artistic work. You can see on campuses all the time what happens with promotions: you move up, up, up, until you are in administration, and it uses up everything you've got. The artist must build a structure, not in the way of being of service to society, but in the way of discovering the dynamism of the interior.

To do that, to keep up with your responsibilities and your fitness and still nurture your creative aspect, you must put a hermetically sealed retort, so that there is no intrusion, around a certain number of hours each day—however many you can honestly afford—and that time must be inviolate. You can allow yourself a few more hours than you think you deserve, but you must make certain you have enough energy and time left over to attend to whatever you have to take care of.

It's like doing your exercises: you set aside a time when you're going to exercise, and that is a holy time. With your art, you should do the same: give a certain number of hours a day to your art, and make it consistent. Then, whether you're writing or not, sit there for those hours: it's a meditation on communication and expression, the two factors in the art work. What will happen, ideally, is that gradually—and it might not be this week or next or even this year—as your given responsibilities drop off, there will be an expansion of the time available to you for the practice of your art. The point I'm making is that your work—that is, your art—and your job must not contaminate each other.

The creative adventure is always reckless. That goes even for the simple thing I do in writing a book. Friedrich Schiller, a German poet in Goethe's time, wrote an interesting letter to a young writer who had writer's block—that's refusal of the call in a writer. Schiller said in the letter, "Your problem is that you bring in the critical factor before the lyric factor has had a chance to express itself." In poetry, for example, we spend our youth studying Shakespeare and Milton, and then, when we start to write our own pitiful little poem, we think, "Oh, my god."

> When writing,
> don't criticize the words coming out.
> Just let them come.
> Let go of the critical factor:
> Will I make money? Am I wasting time?

My writing is of a very different kind from anything I have heard about. All this mythological material is out there, a big gathering of stuff, and I have been reading it for some forty- or fifty-odd years. There are various ways of handling that. The most common is to put the material together and publish a scholarly book about it. But when I'm writing, I try to get a sense of an experiential relationship to the material. In fact, I can't write unless that happens. It is like putting it into some kind of meat grinder that grinds it into a new thing and yet does not do violence to the material. It's very exciting when it comes together that way.

I don't write unless the stuff is really working on me, and my selection of material depends on what works. Usually, with mythology, you are almost cheating, because it is all in shape anyhow. All the elementary ideas are there. You only have to recognize them, and the work cooks. It's the damnedest thing: you are going along, and suddenly you find you have said things you did not know you were saying, because it is all right there.

When I'm writing, I think of the whole academic world: I know how they think about this material, and it is not the same way that I think about it. I just have to say, "Let the guillotine come down. You are still going to have this message." I always feel as if I am going through the Clashing Rocks, and they are just about to close, but I manage to get through before I let that thought overcome me. It's a very strange process: actually holding that door open and getting the sentences out. Do not think about the negative side. There will be negatives that are going to come down, but you have to hold the door open if you are going to do anything that has not been done before. You have to suspend all criticism to do your work. In writing, you have to do this all the time in order to get the sentence out. Suspending criticism is killing the dragon Thou Shalt. Kill him.

> Get the writing out first.
> Forget the critic and just write.
> Afterward, you can bring in
> the critical factor and prune.

If you have trouble because you are thinking, "Who is ever going to see this?"—then think of someone you know who would resonate to your statement and write for that person. It is a great facilitator to have a specific person in mind, until you no longer need an audience. Think of little children, for example, with their tiny eyes looking up at you. Talk to them. Write to them. In a book, you will often see a sincere dedication to the person for whom the book was written. *Alice's Adventures in Wonderland*, for instance, was written for one specific little girl. When I started writing, I thought of my students at Sarah Lawrence, the actual people with whom I was dealing. I knew their thinking and the kinds of words that spoke to them.

The two things, then, that I'd say are necessary for breaking through what's called writer's block are, first, to have a person to whom you are addressing yourself and, second, to set aside a couple of hours a day when, as it were, you're writing letters of love to that person.

> Writer's block results from
> too much head. Cut off your head.
> Pegasus, poetry, was born of Medusa
> when her head was cut off.
> You have to be reckless when writing.
> Be as crazy as your conscience allows.

When you begin to get a sense of the material dictating the form, you will be writing. It may happen fast, or it may take you a little while to find the flow. When I started *The Masks of God*, I dashed off the first book, *Primitive Mythology*. I was in a great hurry to get finished, because I had been given some money to go to Japan for a big session of the International Congress for the History of Religions, so I just churned it out. And then, the reaction to it was so impressive to me—it was a much better book than I thought I had written—that when I started to write Volume II, I was blocked for awhile, until I said, "Hey, listen, come off it. Stick your neck out and just write the book." I thank God that I had read that letter of Schiller's to the young poet.

In religion, one speaks of the fear of God and the love of God. Fear of God will block you. Love of God will carry you on. If you can do something that you love to do without fear of criticism, you will move. You will find joy in it. You do not have to move more than an inch to feel the joy. Remember, the Buddha's third temptation was *dharma*, duty, doing what people expect you to do. That's the censorship fear.

After you have written something, when you see it in typescript, you will want to fool around with it, because it will be different from the way it was in script. Then, when you are satisfied with the typescript, you send it to the publisher. He accepts it, and when he sends you the galleys, you will want to fool with it again. Every time it appears in a form that is not the one directly out of your hand, you get an objective attitude toward it. In a way, you become the reader instead of the writer, and you see it in a new light. This crafting is part of the process of turning something into a work of art. I think that many people today do not realize what it means to be an artist, instead of simply a person who is writing. I mean, there is a craft and an attitude and a willingness to recognize that, unless it is in form, it is not art.

> Let your darlings out,
> but murder them,
> or two years later,
> you'll wish you had.

If you are going to stay in the village compound, the town will take care of you. But if you go on the adventure, it is prudent to go at the right time. This is a real problem if you are overcome late in life, if you have already taken on responsibilities when the light goes on: like Gauguin ,who made a total mess, not only of his life, but of his family's life. But as he went to pieces, his art became greater and greater. He did not go into painting seriously until he was around forty-five years old, and then his life was in his paintings. His was a hero's journey, but at a very high price. It is an ironic situation: you'd say he made a mess of it as a man, but as an artist, he was a triumph.

Then there is the experience of coming back with your jewel and nobody wants it: the "don't-throw-your-pearls-before-swine" sort of thing, lest people turn against you. Often there is not a waiting public. You know the story of the artist who is "ahead of his time," the one who is only appreciated a generation-and-a-half later.

During the 40s and 50s, Jean was working with some artists who were way out, and twenty years later they are top people. John Cage, for example, did music for four of her dances and nobody knew Cage. He was doing the most bizarre things, but he just hung on and knew and knew. Now, he is a major figure in the field.

He also said, "Fame is of no importance." The light of fame comes past, and one may be in it for three minutes, for thity minutes, or never at all. But fame is not what the artist is working for. It's the commercial artist who says, "Whatever they want, I am going to give it to them." The real artist gives expression to a gift that has come to him, and the susception of the gift implies, "I have to put it out."

Sometimes, however, an artist becomes so enraptured by the creative plunge, that you might say "life drops off." This is one of the problems in yoga also. When illumination hits, life drops off, and you can't get back. That's the effect that follows one who is an artist but has not gotten the realization into his or her life.

> In loving the spiritual,
> you cannot despise the earthly.

Joyce was such a person: my god, what a life! When you read Richard Ellman's *James Joyce*, his biography, you wonder how anyone could have lived such a life. You don't know how that man stood it, how his family stood it, how any of his friends stood it. But look what he accomplished. I mean, if you have the eyes to see it.

It took him twelve years to finish *A Portrait of the Artist as a Young Man*. He began the project as an essay in 1904, but the novel wasn't published until 1916. And if Yeats had not recommended him to Ezra Pound, who got him published, we would never have heard of Joyce. Meanwhile, he had written *Dubliners* and was at work on *Ulysses*, which he spent seven years writing. It's as though he said, "There it is. I have to formulate this thing for my own realization of what it is."

The first editions of *Ulysses* were burned by New York and English customs authorities I think only one or two copies remain. Finally, he had to have it printed in France, and when I was a student, that was the only place you could buy *Ulysses*. People here in the United States did not even know it existed.

He spent sixteen years writing *Finnegans Wake*, and you should have read the reviews when that came out: "What is this guy doing? Has he gone nuts? Is he just pulling a crazy job on us?" The first edition of *Finnegans Wake* was remaindered within two months. I bought four hardcover copies for fifty-six cents each. When a book is remaindered, the publisher is trying to get back the money for printing it. The author gets nothing.

Joyce died three weeks short of his fifty-ninth birthday, with the final book he was planning left undone. He would not be my model for a life, but he is a model for my relationship to art. Thomas Mann said Joyce was probably the greatest novelist of the twentieth century. But, look what it cost him to do that.

Joyce endured all these travails because his intention was perfection. Perfection is the fulfillment implicit in art, and he achieved it. Imperfection is life. All forms in life are imperfect, but the function of art is to see the radiance through the imperfection.

> The artist opens
> the forms of the work
> to transcendence.

What I understand art to be, then, is the revealing power of maya: the production in music, in dance, in the visual arts, and in literature of such "divinely superfluous beauty," of objects for esthetic arrest which are of no practical use, but which open up dimensions within. And the projecting power of maya, on the other hand, I take to be desire and loathing, which link you in phenomenal discourse to the object as object. It is as clear and clean as that.

In India, there are two orders of art: one is esthetic art; the other, temple art, is not esthetic in its aim. Temple art is concerned not with arresting the eye but with affecting a psychic transformation in the artist and the beholder. We're into another kind of art here. The source of the image is a vision. Europeans for quite a while had a hard time appreciating Indian art. Indian poetry and philosophy were appreciated, but not the art, until they realized the images weren't representations of things, but tools for psychic transformation.

Now, with Joyce, I would say *Finnegans Wake* is a book that affects a psychic transformation in the reader. If the reader really works on it and finds out what Joyce is saying, there is a vision there that can transform one's relationship to the world.

Coomaraswamy has given considerable attention to the conception of an Indian religious work of art. Let us say an artist is going to do something on Shiva in the dance. First he studies the textbooks on Shiva: what the organization of the image should be, what should be in the god's hands, and all that. Then he pronounces the god's name, meditates, and brings forth in his own consciousness an image of the god dancing, so that what is presented has been derived from inner, rather than from outer, vision.

Normally we look at the Nataraja Shiva with an esthetic intent: we see it simply as an art object. But the one who is devoted to Shiva lets that object become an opening of those centers in his own consciousness that correspond to the Shiva in himself: "I am Shiva." That is very different from just looking at a Shiva image.

One is often unable to experience Indian temple art in an esthetic way at all, because it has intended another kind of effect. You have to move into the god position to grasp what the image has given you. Indian temple art is not pornographic, because you are not excited to desire the object depicted. Say you go to an art gallery desiring to have an esthetic experience. It is static, and insofar as it affects a transformation of consciousness, it brings about a new stasis within you. There is a transformation just as there is a transformation with esthetic arrest. You are no longer the lecherous human being. You are stabilized in esthetic arrest. Temple art pushes that one dimension further, so that your consciousness with respect to all things in the world is changed. It's a permanent change that takes place in you. Perhaps one could say that all true art is temple art, but there is a difference between art that intends esthetic arrest and art that intends psychic transformation. You could say the latter is not properly art. It is a religious device.

Some artists are in pain, others are not. Picasso had a run of wives and women that was just fantastic. What one wife did would not have mattered a bit. I do not think it possible to interpret Picasso's life as one of pain. In the Picasso Retrospective, which I saw twice at the Museum of Modern Art, there was one room filled with about twenty-five paintings that he had done in one day. What was it that impelled him to this fury of action? He was certainly the type of artist in whom life is so abundant that the art is easily handled, which shows the great skill of his nature.

I read Wagner's autobiography—fantastic! That guy was writing three operas, carrying on three love affairs, and actually being resentful that the women's husbands would not give money to help produce his operas! He was outta sight! His knowledge of mythology was way ahead of what any of the scholars in his time knew. In the Ring Cycle, he combined into one unit two aspects of Germanic mythology: the hero journey and the cosmic order—coming into the world and going out of the world. On top of that, at the same time he was writing the librettos, he amplified the orchestra to such an extent—using reeds and French horns and so on—that he effectively invented a whole new orchestra! And he designed what is probably the best theatre that Europe has had. I can't understand how he did it all. I think some people just have so much spunk that they cannot be judged in ordinary terms.

I never knew an artist who didn't want money, but they don't pursue it. Their minds are elsewhere. Joyce begged everyone he knew for money. But he couldn't make money and do what he did: sixteen years writing *Finnegans Wake*. Bringing that prodigious load into the "room of his life" was all that Joyce could manage.

Schiller, a sensitive and intelligent student of psychology in relation to art, distinguished two types of artists: one, he called the "sentimental" artist; the other, the "naive" artist. He used as his models Goethe and himself. He was the sentimental artist: the one without great means, who did not pay proper attention to his health, for whom art was his life, not the other way around. *Everything* went into his art. Goethe, on the other hand, was the naive artist: a man of ample life, an important person in local politics, a person for whom art was but one aspect of his life. Some such people require a bit more instruction than others, but Goethe had fantastic intuition, great energy, and vitality. He was a masterly artist.

Thomas Mann wrote an interesting paper called "Goethe and Tolstoy," based on this idea of Schiller's. He compared Dostoevsky to the sentimental artist, as Schiller had described himself, and Tolstoy to the naive artist. Tolstoy was a property owner, who used to put on a nice silk shirt, go out, and harvest the grain with his peasants. He would make believe he was a peasant, but that was all part of the game too.

It's interesting to compare the works of these two types of writers. The Schiller-Dostoevsky types tend to be highly hopped up. There's a strong, dramatic conflict in their writing. Both Tolstoy and Goethe, on the other hand, are genial authors, and their works have powerful passages of epic proportions and a wonderful majesty. Conversely, in Dostoevsky's *Crime and Punishment* it is pain, pain—a life of inward, spiritual agony. These are two different ways, two different temperaments. The pain is not something sentimental artists strive for, it results from their giving all of their energy to divinely superfluous activity and not paying attention to the living of life.

We are to fill the sacred space, then, with art. And when I say "art," I mean "divinely superfluous beauty," not doodling and having pretty decorations in your house. The sacred space is where things are experienced as not being of any practical use. It is through the contemplation of something "thus come"—"divinely superfluous"—that the aspects of oneself that are not of immediate practical use can come forth. I think organic growth comes in that way, not in the way of going into a practical activity.

The practical activity comes after the organism has stated itself in its maturity, or else it comes forth in a distorted way: the person thinks of himself as nothing but a plumber or something like that. That's the problem in a traditional culture like India, where people from birth are cookie-molded into the *dharma* of their caste. And they are nothing but that. They never become human beings, individuals, but remain dividuals: people that are elements in a larger structure.

I think that is the big difference between the Oriental and the Occidental ideal for a human being. The person in the Orient is either a warrior, or a merchant, or whatever, and nothing else. In the West, however, the person is an individual. The Greeks had the idea of the total individual and held it up as being completely different from the Oriental idea of people being trained into a pattern of life in accordance with the necessities of society. I experienced this idea of the total individual at Delphi, where you see everything related: the oracle, the art, the theatre, and the stadium up on top.

For most people, the life of art is an all-absorbing matter, and it requires a hell of a lot of work. What Ramakrishna said about illumination is also true about art: "Unless you seek it as a man whose hair is on fire seeks a pond, don't pursue it." It is too difficult.

For women who marry, it requires a hell of an acquiescence on the part of the husband, too—I can tell you about that. I know so many young women who were in dance, then married, and the husband could not stand it. And, of course, it is difficult to have a family with an art that requires the kind of discipline dance demands. The thing about dance is that if you are not disciplined, it is damned evident the next time you get on stage.

Jean once said, "The way of the artist and the way of the mystic are similar, but the mystic lacks a craft." The craft keeps the artist in touch with the phenomenality *of* the world and in a relationship *to* it: a constant evaluation of the uniqueness of each event in the world. The mystic, by contrast, can be so darned abstract that there is no link to life except the begging bowl. Yet, sometimes those begging bowls can be very productive. Some of our gurus are pulling in millions of dollars. But that does not mean they are related to life.

I have seen the training of artists in this country and in Europe. They are trained only in the craft. They are given techniques for rendering something, but they do not know what to do with the techniques. I've know many of them who just cracked up. Their art technique becomes a wall they cannot penetrate, so they try to think of anecdotes and narratives to render that show off their technique. They are so loaded with sociology, that they think they do not have an art object if there is not some kind of lesson in there for fixing the world or themselves. But, in fact, an art object by definition is "divinely superfluous beauty."

Do you see in this the projecting power of maya and the revealing power? As long as the motifs of desire and loathing are moving you, it is the projecting aspect.

You are yourself the maya-maker, and you are the one who opens the revealing power when your attitude is that of the Buddha. When I realized this, it was thrilling to me. I think that art and this knowledge of what art is can be the modern Western way to illumination. It will release you from all kinds of linkages. It will not keep you from practicing all those things you hardly believe in, but it will help you in achieving the esthetic before you become linked to the objects of your life.

> When you distinguish
> between good and evil,
> you've lost the art.

> Art goes beyond morality.

> The reach of your compassion
> is the reach of your art.

JOYCE'S trick was seeing symbols everywhere.

...Dr. John W. Perry has characterized the living myth-ological symbol as an "affect image." It is an image that hits one where it counts. It is not addressed first to the brain, to be there interpreted and appreciated. On the contrary, if that is where it has to be read, the symbol is already dead. An "affect image" talks directly to the feeling system and immediately elicits a response, after which the brain may come along with its interesting comments. There is some kind of throb of res-onance within, responding to the image shown without, like the answer of a musical string to another equally tuned. And so it is that when the vital symbols of any given social group evoke in all its members responses of this kind, a sort of ma-gical accord unites them as one spiritual organism, functioning through members who, though separate in space, are yet one in being and belief.[143]

Once you understand symbolic things,
you, too, will see symbols everywhere.

The wonder is that the characteristic efficacy to touch and inspire deep creative centers dwells in the smallest nursery fairy tale—as the flavor of the ocean is contained in a droplet or the whole mystery of life within the egg of a flea. For the symbols of mythology are not manufactured; they cannot be ordered, invented, or permanently suppressed. They are spontaneous productions of the psyche, and each bears within it, undamaged, the germ power of its source.[144]

> The divine manifestation is ubiquitous,
> only our eyes are not open to it.

> The symbol opens our eyes.

"A true symbol takes us to the center of the circle, not to another point on the circumference. It is by symbolism that man enters effectively and consciously into contact with his own deepest self, with other men, and with God...."
—*Thomas Merton*[145]

> Frequently a symbol doesn't open
> our eyes, but closes them instead.

> If we oncretize the symbol,
> we get stuck with it.

In short, then: just as the buffalo suddenly disappeared from the North American plains, leaving the Indians deprived not only of a central mythic symbol but also of the very manner of life that the symbol once had served, so likewise in our own beautiful world, not only have our public religious symbols lost their claim to authority and passed away, but the ways of life they once supported have also disappeared; and as the Indians then turned inward, so do many in our own baffled world—and frequently with Oriental, not Occidental, guidance in this potentially very dangerous, often ill-advised interior adventure, questing within for the affect images that our secularized social order with its incongruously archaic religious institutions can no longer render.[146]

The world has been desanctified.

The chick from the egg
is a symbol of the spirit of Easter.

The image of the cosmic egg is known to many myth-ologies; it appears in the Greek Orphic, Egyptian, Finnish, Buddhistic, and Japanese. "In the beginning this world was merely nonbeing," we read in a sacred work of the Hindus; "It was existent. It developed. It turned into an egg. It lay for the period of a year. It was split asunder. One of the two parts became silver, one gold. That which was of silver is the earth. That which is of gold is the sky. What was the outer membrane is the mountains. What was the inner mem-brane is cloud and mist. What were the veins are the rivers. What was the fluid within is the ocean. Now, what was born therefrom is yonder sun."[147] The shell of the cosmic egg is the world frame of space, while the fertile seed-power within typifies the inexhaustible life dynamism of nature.[148]

The eggshell is cast off by the chick, as the skin is sloughed off by the serpent, or the shadow of the moon is shed by the moon reborn.

> Snake and moon both die to the old,
> shedding their shadows to be reborn.

Birds in flight and Christ on the cross: both sym-bolize the spirit released from the bondage of earth. The moon, like Christ, dies and is resurrected. The moon is three nights dark: Jesus was three nights in the grave with a stone covering the cave entrance—the dark disk over the moon. The dating of Easter according to both lunar and solar calendars suggests that life, like the light reborn in the moon and eternal in the sun, finally *is* one. The whole mystery is right there in Christian symbology.

The moon, furthermore, and the spectacle of the night sky, the stars and the Milky Way, have constituted, certainly from the beginning, a source of wonder and profound impression. But there is actually a physical influence of the moon upon the earth and its creatures, its tides and our own interior tides, which has long been consciously recognized as well as subliminally experienced. The coincidence of the menstrual cycle with that of the moon is a physical actuality structuring human life and a curiosity that has been observed with wonder. It is in fact likely that the fundamental notion of a life-structuring relationship between the heavenly world and that of man was derived from the realization, both in experience and in thought, of the force of the lunar cycle. The mystery, also, of the death and resurrection of the moon, as well as of its influence on dogs, wolves and foxes, jackals and coyotes, which try to sing to it: this immortal silver dish of wonder, cruising among the beautiful stars and racing through the clouds, turning waking life itself into a sort of dream, has been a force and presence even more powerful in the shaping of mythology than the sun, by which its light and its world of stars, night sounds, erotic modes, and the magic of dream, are daily quenched.[149]

Dew is an ambrosia
fallen from the moon.

This lunar symbology is ancient: the moon god in Mesopotamia was named Sin; the mountain that Moses ascended was Mount Sinai. It may have been the moon goddess mountain. When Moses came down from that mountain, he was so luminous from his reception of God's energy that he wore a veil in front of his face, and emenating from his forehead were horns of light: the horns of the lunar mystery.

"The moon lives twenty-eight days and this is our month. Each of these days represents something sacred to us: two of the days represent the Great Spirit; two are for Mother Earth; four are for the four winds; one is for the Spotted Eagle; one for the sun; and one for the moon; one is for the Morning Star; and four are for the four ages; seven for our seven great rites; one is for the buffalo; one for the fire; one for the water; one for the rock; and finally, one is for the two-legged people. If you add all these days up you will see that they come to twenty-eight. You should know also that the buffalo has twenty-eight ribs, and that in our war bonnets we usually wear twenty-eight feathers. You see, there is a significance for everything, and these are things that are good for men to know and to remember."—Black Elk[150]

Awe is what moves us forward.

...in the contemporary world of cross-cultural communication, where the minds of men, leaping the local fences, can recognize common fields of experience and realization under alien forms, what many priests and sociologists regard as eight distinct deities, the comparative mythologist and psychologist can take to be aspects of one and the same....[151]

Myth deities personify energies
that are around us in nature.

The gods and goddesses then are to be understood as embodiments and custodians of the elixir of Imperishable Being but not themselves the Ultimate in its primary state. What the hero seeks through his intercourse with them is therefore not finally themselves, but their grace, i.e., the power of their sustaining substance. This miraculous energy-substance and this alone is the Imperishable....[152]

Live from your own center.

The key to understanding the problem that's solved with the symbolic idea of the Trinity is the Tantric saying, "To worship a god, one must become a god." That is to say, you must hit that level of consciousness within yourself that is equivalent to the deity to whom you are addressing your attention.

In the Trinity, the Father is the deity your attention is addressed to; you are the Son, knower of the Father; and the Holy Spirit represents the relationship between the two.

It seems to me you cannot have the notion of a god without having implicit the notion of a Trinity: a god, the knower of the god, and the relationship between the two, a progressive knowing that brings you closer and closer to the divine.

The divine lives within you.

...there is still one more degree of realization...namely that termed in Japanese "ji ji mu ge"—"thing and thing, no division": no separation between things: the analogy suggested is of a net of gems: the universe as a great spread-out net with at every joint a gem, and each gem not only reflecting all the others but itself reflected in all. An alternate image is of a wreath of flowers. In a wreath, no flower is the "cause" of any other, yet together, all are the wreath.[153]

The separateness
apparent in the world
is secondary.

The very great physicist Erwin Schrödinger has made the same metaphysical point in his startling and sublime little book, My View of the World. *"All of us living beings belong together," he there declares, "in as much as we are all in reality sides or aspects of one single being, which may perhaps in western terminology be called God while in the Upanishads its name is Brahman."*[154]

Beyond the world of opposites
is an unseen, but experienced,
unity and identity in us all.

For we are all, in every particle of our being, precipitations of consciousness; as are, likewise, the animals and plants, metals cleaving to a magnet and waters tiding to the moon.[155]

Today the planet is
the only proper "in group."

...we are to recognize in this whole universe a reflection magnified of our own most inward nature; so that we are indeed its ears, its eyes, its thinking, and its speech—or, in theological terms, God's ears, God's eyes, God's thinking, and God's Word; and, by the same token, participants here and now in an act of creation that is continuous in the whole infinitude of that space of our mind through which the planets fly, and our fellows of earth now among them.[156]

Participate joyfully
in the sorrows of the world.

The obvious lesson...is that the first step to the knowl-edge of the highest divine symbol of the wonder and mystery of life is in the recognition of the monstrous nature of life and its glory in that character: the realization that this is just how it is and that it cannot and will not be changed. Those who think—and their name is legion—that they know how the universe could have been better than it is, how it would have been had they created it, without pain, without sorrow, with-out time, without life, are unfit for illumination. Or those who think—as do many— "Let me first correct society, then get around to myself" are barred from even the outer gate of the mansion of God's peace. All societies are evil, sorrowful, inequitable; and so they will always be. So if you really want to help this world, what you will have to teach is how to live in it. And that no one can do who has not himself learned how to live in it in the joyful sorrow and sorrowful joy of the knowledge of life as it is.[157]

We cannot cure the world of sorrows,
but we can choose to live in joy.

Flying down from Boston to New York at night, the plane goes over highly populated areas and you can see rivers of automobile lights, like blood molecules going through the veins. You really get a sense of this whole thing as a strange organism. The life of the planet depends on certain areas in the swamplands and so forth that are being violated now. People who don't have a concept of the whole can do very unfortunate things in neighborhood development.

"If those who lead you say to you: 'See, the Kingdom is in heaven,' then the birds of the heaven will precede you. If they say to you: 'It is in the sea,' then the fish will precede you. But the Kingdom is within you and it is without you. If you will know yourselves, then you will be known and you will know that you are the sons of the Living Father. But if you do not know yourselves, then you are in poverty and you are poverty." —Jesus Christ[158]

> You must return
> with the bliss
> and integrate it.

Every now and then, while I'm walking along Fifth Avenue, everything just breaks up into subatomic particles and I think, "Well, Jesus Christ, that *is* what it is. This is the experience of maya, an illusion of the senses if there ever was one." It's a fantastic thought.

His disciples said to Him: "When will the Kingdom come?" Jesus said: "It will not come by expectation; they will not say: 'See, here' or: 'See there.' But the Kingdom of the Father is spread upon the earth and men do not see it."[159]

> The return is seeing
> the radiance everywhere.

"The president in Washington sends word that he wishes to buy our land. But how can you buy or sell the sky? The land? The idea is strange to us. If we do not own the freshness of the air and the sparkle of the water, how can you buy them?

"Every part of this earth is sacred to my people. Every single pine needle, every sandy shore, every mist in the dark woods, every meadow, every humming insect. All are holy in the memory and experience of my people.

"We know the sap which courses through the trees as we know the blood that courses through our veins. We are part of the earth and it is part of us. The perfumed flowers are our sisters. The bear, the deer, the great eagle, these are our brothers. The rocky crests, the juices in the meadow, the body heat of the pony, and man, all belong to the same family.

"The shining water that moves in the streams and rivers is not just water, but the blood of our ancestors. If we sell you our land, you must remember that it is sacred. Each ghostly reflection in the clear water of the lakes tells of events and memories in the life of my people. The water's murmur is the voice of my father's father.

"The rivers are our brothers. They quench our thirst. They carry our canoes and feed our children. So you must give to the rivers the kindness you would give any brother.

"If we sell you our land, remember that the air is precious to us, that the air shares its spirit with all the life it supports. The wind that gave our grandfather his first breath also receives his last sigh. The wind also gives our children the spirit of life. So if we sell you our land, you must keep it apart and sacred, as a place where man can go to taste the wind that is sweetened by the meadow flowers.

"Will you teach your children what we have taught our children? That the earth is our mother? What befalls the earth befalls all the sons of the earth.

"This we know: The earth does not belong to man, man belongs to the earth. All things are connected like the blood which unites us all. Man did not weave the web of life, he is merely a strand in it. Whatever he does to the web, he does to himself.

"One thing we know: our god is also your god. The earth is precious to him and to harm the earth is to heap contempt on its creator.

"Your destiny is a mystery to us. What will happen when the buffalo are all slaughtered? The wild horses tamed? What will happen when the secret corners of the forest are heavy with the scent of many men and the view of the ripe hills is blotted by talking wires? Where will the thicket be? Gone! Where will the eagle be? Gone! And what is it to say goodbye to the swift pony and the hunt? The end of living and the beginning of survival.

"When the last Red Man has vanished with his wilderness and his memory is only the shadow of a cloud moving across the prairie, will these shores and forests still be here? Will there be any of the spirit of my people left?

"We love this earth as a newborn loves its mother's heartbeat. So, if we sell you our land, love it as we have loved it. Care for it as we have cared for it. Hold in your mind the memory of the land as it is when you receive it. Preserve the land for all children and love it, as God loves us all.

"As we are part of the land, you too are part of the land. This earth is precious to us. It is also precious to you. One thing we know: There is only one God. No man, be he Red Man or White Man can be apart. We are brothers after all."
—Chief Seattle[160]

The world is a match for us.
We are a match for the world.

*Having soared beyond thought into boundless space,
circled many times the arid moon, and begun their long
return: how welcome a sight, [the astronauts] said, was the
beauty of their goal, this planet Earth, "like an oasis in the
desert of infinite space!" Now there is a telling image: this
earth—the one oasis in all space, an extraordinary kind of
sacred grove, as it were, set apart for the rituals of life; and not
simply one part or section of this earth, but the entire globe
now a sanctuary, a set-apart Blessed Place. Moreover, we
have all now seen for ourselves how very small is our heaven-
born earth, and how perilous our position on the surface of its
whirling, luminously beautiful orb.*[161]

*...we are the children of this beautiful planet that we
have lately seen photographed from the moon. We were not
delivered into it by some god, but have come forth from it.*[162]

The spirit is the bouquet of nature.

*We may think of ourselves, then, as the functioning ears
and eyes and minds of this earth, exactly as our own ears and
eyes and minds are of our bodies. Our bodies are one with
this earth, this wonderful "oasis in the desert of infinite
space"; and the mathematics of that infinite space, which are
the same as of Newton's mind—our mind, the earth's mind,
the mind of the universe—come to flower and fruit in this
beautiful oasis through ourselves.*[163]

The first function of mythology
is to sanctify the place you are in.

"The world," wrote the poet Rilke, "is large, but in us it is deep as the sea." We carry the laws within us by which it is held in order. And we ourselves are no less mysterious. In searching out its wonders, we are learning simultaneously the wonder of ourselves. That moon flight as an outward journey was outward into ourselves. And I do not mean this poetically, but factually, historically. I mean that the actual fact of the making and the visual broadcasting of that trip has transformed, deepened, and extended human consciousness to a degree and in a manner that amounts to the opening of a new spiritual era.

...that lovely satellite has been out there circling our earth for some four billion years like a beautiful but lone-some woman trying to catch earth's eye. She has now at last caught it, and has caught thereby ourselves. And as always happens when a temptation of that kind has been responded to, a new life has opened, richer, more exciting and fulfilling, for both of us than was known, or even thought of or imagined, before. There are youngsters among us, even now, who will be living on that moon; others who will visit Mars. And their sons? What voyages are to be theirs?[164]

Follow your bliss.

What is, or what is to be, the new mythology? Since myth is of the order of poetry, let us ask first a poet: Walt Whitman, for example, in his Leaves of Grass *(1855):*

> *"I have said that the soul is not more than the body,*
> *And I have said that the body is not more than the soul,*
> *And nothing, not God, is greater to one than one's-*
>   *self is,*
> *And whoever walks a furlong without sympathy walks*
>   *to his own funeral, dressed in his shroud,*
> *And I or you pocketless of a dime may purchase the pick*
>   *of the earth,*

And to glance with an eye or show a bean in its pod
    confounds the learning of all times,
And there is no trade or employment but the young man
    following it may become a hero,
And there is no object so soft but it makes a hub for the
    wheeled universe,
And any man or woman shall stand cool and
    supercilious before a million universes.

And I call to mankind, Be not curious about God,
For I who am curious about each am not curious
    about God,
No array of terms can say how much I am at peace about
    God and about death.

I hear and behold God in every object, yet I understand
    God not in the least,
Nor do I understand who there can be more wonderful
    than myself.

Why should I wish to see God better than this day?
I see something of God each hour of the twenty-four,
    and each moment then,
In the faces of men and women I see God, and in my
    own face in the glass;
I find letters from God dropped in the street, and every
    one is signed by God's name,
And I leave them where they are, for I know that others
    will punctually come forever and ever."[165]

These lines of Whitman echo marvelously the sentiments
of the earliest of the Upanishads, the "Great Forest Book"
(Brihadaranyaka) of about the eighth century B.C.

"This that people say, 'Worship this god! Worship that
god!'—one god after another! All this is his creation indeed!
And he himself is all the gods....He is entered in the universe even to our fingernail-tips, like a razor in a razor case,

or fire in firewood. Him those people see not, for as seen he is incomplete. When breathing, he becomes 'breath' by name; when speaking, 'voice'; when seeing, 'the eye'; when hearing, 'the ear'; when thinking, 'mind': these are but the names of his acts....

"One should worship with the thought that he is one's self, for therein all these become one. This self is the footprint of that All, for by it one knows the All—just as, verily, by following a footprint one finds cattle that have been lost.... One should reverence the Self alone as dear. And he who reverences the Self alone as dear—what he holds dear, verily, will not perish....

So whosoever worships another divinity than his self, thinking, 'He is one, I am another,' knows not. He is like a sacrificial animal for the gods...."[166]

Indeed, do we not hear the same from Christ himself, as reported in the early *Gnostic* Gospel According to Thomas?

"Whoever drinks from my mouth shall become as I am and I myself will become he, and the hidden things shall be revealed to him....I am the All, the All came forth from me and the All attained to me. Cleave a piece of wood, I am there; lift up the stone and you will find me there."[167]

If you want the whole thing,
the gods will give it to you.
But you must be ready for it.

There are now no more horizons. And with the dissolution of horizons we have experienced and are experiencing collisions, terrific collisions, not only of peoples but also of their mythologies. It is as when dividing panels are withdrawn from between chambers of very hot and very cold airs: there is a rush of these forces together....That is just what we are experiencing; and we are riding it: riding it to a new age, a new birth, a totally new condition of mankind—to which no one anywhere alive today can say that he has the key, the answer, the prophecy, to its dawn. Nor is there anyone to condemn here...What is occurring is completely natural, as are its pains, confusions, and mistakes.[168]

The goal is to live
with godlike composure
on the full rush of energy,
like Dionysus riding the leopard,
without being torn to pieces.

Mythologies, in other words, mythologies and religions are great poems and, when recognized as such, point infallibly through things and events to the ubiquity of a "presence" or "eternity" that is whole and entire in each. In this function all mythologies, all great poetries, and all mystic traditions are in accord; and where any such inspiriting vision remains effective in a civilization, everything and every creature within its range is alive. The first condition, therefore, that any mythology must fulfill if it is to render life to modern lives is that of cleansing the doors of perception to the wonder, at once terrible and fascinating, of ourselves and of the universe of which we are the ears and eyes and the mind.[169]

> A bit of advice
> given to a young Native American
> at the time of his initiation:
>
> "As you go the way of life,
> you will see a great chasm.
>
> Jump.
>
> It is not as wide as you think."

And so, to return to our opening question: What is—or what is to be—the new mythology?

It is—and will forever be, as long as our human race exists—the old, everlasting, perennial mythology, in its "subjective sense," poetically renewed in terms neither of a remembered past nor of a projected future, but of now: addressed, that is to say, not to the flattery of "peoples," but to the waking of individuals in the knowledge of themselves, not simply as egos fighting for place on the surface of this beautiful planet, but equally as centers of Mind at Large— each in his own way at one with all...[170]

Notes

[1]M. Capek, *The Philosophical Impact of Contemporary Physics* (Princeton, NJ: D. Van Nostrand, 1961), p. 319; as cited in Fritjof Capra, *The Tao of Physics* (Boulder, CO: 1975), p. 211.

[2]Joseph Campbell, *Creative Mythology*, Vol. 4 of *The Masks of God* (New York: Viking Penguin Inc., 1968), p. 508.

[3]This paragrah is paraphrased and quoted from C. G. Jung, *The Structure and Dynamics of the Psyche, The Collected Works of C. G. Jung*, Bollingen Series XX, Vol. 8, pars. 789–792; originally published as "Die seelischen Probleme der menschlichen Altersufen," *Neue Zürcher Zeitung*, March 14 and 16, 1930; Revised, largely rewritten, and republished as "Die Lebenswende," *Seelenprobleme der Gegenwart* (Psychologische Abhandlunger, III; Zurich, 1931), which version was translated by W. S. Dell and Cary F. Baynes as "The Stages of Life," *Modern Man in Search of a Soul* (London and New York, 1933); the present translation by R. F. C. Hull is based on this; acited in *The Portable Jung*, edited by Joseph Campbell (New York: Viking Penguin Inc., 1970), pp. 19–20.

[4]Matthew 18:3.

[5]Morris E. Opler, "Myths and Tales of the Jicarilla Apache Indians," in *Memoirs of the American Folklore Society,* Vol. XXXI (1938,) p. 110.

[6]Walt Whitman, "Song of the Open Road," in *Leaves of Grass*

[7]Joseph Campbell, *Myths to Live By* (New York: Viking Penguin Inc., 1972), pp. 23–24.

[8]Brihadarnayaka Upanishad 1.4.1–5.; quoted in Joseph Campbell, *Primitive Mythology*, Vol. 1 of *The Masks of God* (New York: Viking Penguin Inc., 1959), p. 105.

[9]*Primitive Mythology*, op. cit., p. 104; abridging *Symposium* 189D ff, from *The Dialogues of Plato*, translated by Benjamin Jowett (London: Oxford University Press, 1953).

[10]C. G. Jung, *Axion: Researches into the Phenomenology of the Self, The Collected Works of C. G. Jung*, op. cit., Vol. 9, Part II, par. 26; translated by R. F. C. Hull (New York: Bollingen Foundation, 1959) from the first part of *Axion: Untersuchungen zur*

Symbolgeschichte, Psychologische Abhandlungen, VIII (Zurich: Rascher Verlag, 1951); cited in *The Portable Jung,* op. cit., p. 151.

[11]Ibid., pars. 28–30, abr.; cited in *The Portable Jung,* op. cit., pp. 152–153, abr.

[12]Erik Routley, *The Man for Others* (New York: Oxford University Press, 1964), p. 99; cited in *Creative Mythology,* op. cit., p. 177.

[13]Gurraut de Borneilh, *Tam cum los oills el cor....,* in John Rutherford, The Troubadors (London: Smith, Elder and Company, 1861), pp. 34–35; cited in *Creative Mythology,* op. cit., pp. 177–178.

[14]*Creative Mythology,* op. cit., p. 567; Campbell here paraphrases James Joyce, *A Portrait of the Artist as a Young Man* (London: Jonathen Cape, Ltd., 1916), p. 196.

[15]Joseph Campbell, *The Hero with a Thousand Faces,* Bollingen XVII, 2nd edition, revised (Princeton, N.J.: Princeton University Press, 1976), p. 228.

[16]Arthur Schopenhauer, "Die beiden Grundproblemen der Ethik," II. "Über das Fundament der Moral" (1840), *Sämtliche Werke,* 12 Vols. (Stuttgart: Verlag der Cotta'schen Buchhandlung, 1895–1898) Vol. 7, p. 253; cited in Joseph Campbell, *The Inner Reaches of Outer Space* (New York: Alfred van der Marck Editions, 1985; Harper & Row/Perennial Library reprint, 1988), p. 112.

[17]Ibid., p. 254.

[18]*Myths to Live By,* op. cit., p. 155.

[19]Campbell comments: "See Melanie Klein, *The Psychoanalysis of Children,* The International Psycho-Analytical Library, No. 27 (1937)."

[20]Géza Róheim, *War, Crime, and the Covenant* (Journal of Clinical Psychopathology, Monograph Series, No. 1, Monticello, N.Y., 1945), pp. 137–138.

[21]*The Hero with a Thousand Faces,* op. cit., pp. 173–174.

[22]*Myths to Live By,* op. cit., pp. 220–221.

[23]Ibid., p. 47.

[24]Wolfram von Eschenbach, *Parzival* 3.118.14–17 and 28; translated (in part) from Helen M. Mustard and Charles E. Passage (New York: Vintage Books, 1961), p. 127.

[25]Ibid., 3.119.29–30.

[26] Joseph Campbell, *Occidental Mythology*, Vol. 3 of *The Masks of God* (New York: Viking Penguin Inc., 1964), pp. 508–509.

[27] *Creative Mythology*, op. cit., pp. 677–678.

[28] James Joyce, op. cit., p. 247; cited in Joseph Campbell, *The Flight of the Wild Gander: Explorations in the Mythological Dimensions of Fairy Tales, Legends, and Symbols* (New York: HaarperCollins Publishers, 1990), p. 209.

[29] *Myths to Live By*, op. cit., p. 68.

[30] Albert Pauphilet, editor, *La Queste del Saint Graal* (Paris: Champion, 1949), p.26; as cited in *Creative Mythology*, op. cit.

[31] C. G. Jung, *Psychology and Alchemy*, translated by R. F. C. Hull, in *The Collected Works of C. G. Jung*, op. cit., Vol.. 12 (New York: Bollingen Foundation, 1953, 1968), p. 222; cited in *Myths to Live By*, op. cit., p. 68.

[32] Joseph Campbell, "Mythological Themes in Creative Literature and Art," in *Myths, Dreams, and Religion*, edited by Joseph Campbell (New York: E. P. Dutton & Co., Inc., 1970), p. 148.

[33] James Joyce, *A Portrait of the Artist as a Young Man*, op. cit., Penguin ed., p. 203; as cited in "Mythological Themes in Creative Literature and Art," op. cit., p. 168.

[34] Ibid., p. 174.

[35] *The Flight of the Wild Gander*, op. cit., p. 226.

[36] *The Hero with a Thousand Faces*, op. cit., p. 53.

[37] Ibid., p. 17.

[38] Ibid., p. 217.

[39] Ibid., p. 229.

[40] *Myths to Live By*, op. cit., p. 238.

[41] C. G. Jung, *Modern Man in Search of a Soul* (New York: Harcourt, Brace and Company, 1936), p. 129; cited in *Primitive Mythology*, op. cit., p. 124.

[42] Ibid., p. 126; cited in *Primitive Mythology*, op. cit., p. 124.

[43] *Primitive Mythology*, op. cit., p123.

[44] *The Hero with a Thousand Faces*, op. cit., pp. 365–366.

[45] *The Flight of the Wild Gander*, op. cit., p. 110.

[46] *The Hero with a Thousand Faces*, op. cit., p. 121.

[47] Ibid., p. 356.

[48] Ibid., p. 308.

[49]*Myths to Live By*, op. cit., p. 131, abridged.

[50]*Bhagavad Gita*, 2.27, 30, 23; translated, abridged, and reordered by Joseph Campbell and cited in *Myths to Live By*, op. cit., p.202.

[51]Lao-tse, *Tao Teh King*, 16 (translation by Dwight Goddard, *Laotzu's Tao and Wu Wei*; New York, 1919, p. 18; as cited in *The Hero with a Thousand Faces*, op. cit., p. 189.

[52]Ovid, *Metamorphoses*, XV, 252–255; as cited in *The Hero with a Thousand Faces*, op. cit., p. 243.

[53]*The Hero with a Thousand Faces*, op. cit., p. 367.

[54]Arnold J. Toynbee, *A Study of History* (Oxford University Press, 1934), Vol. VI, pp. 169–175, summarized.

[55]*The Hero with a Thousand Faces*, op. cit., p. 16.

[56]Patanjali, *Yoga Sutras* 1.1–2, from Heinrich Zimmer, *Philosophies of India*, edited by Joseph Campbell, Bollingen Series XXVI (New York: Bollingen Foundation, 1951), p. 284.

[57]Joseph Cambell, *The Mythic Image*, Bollingen Series C (Princeton, NJ: Princeton University Press, 1974), p. 313.

[58]Ibid., p. 331.

[59]Ibid., p. 341.

[60]Ibid., p. 345.

[61]Ibid., p. 350.

[62]Ibid., p. 356.

[63]Ibid.

[64]*Meister Eckhart*, edited by Franz Pfeiffer, translated by C. de B. Evans (London: John M. Watkins, 1924–1931), No. XCVI ("Riddance"), I, 239.

[65]*Mandukya Upanisad* 9–11.

[66]*The Flight of the Wild Gander*, op. cit., p. 177.

[67]C. G. Jung, "The Meaning of Psychology for Modern Man," *Civilization in Transition*, in *The Collected Works of C. G. Jung*, op. cit., Vol. 10 (New York: Bollingen Foundation, 1964), pp.. 144–145, ar. 304–305; cited in *The Mythic Image*, op. cit., p. 7, abr.

[68]C. G. Jung, *Analytical Psychology: Its Theory and Practice* (New York: Pantheon Books, 1968), p. 46; cited in *The Mythic Image*, op. cit., p. 186.

[69]*Myths to Live By*, op. cit., p. 219.

[70]Ibid., pp. 217–218.

[71]C. G. Jung, *Analytical Psychology*, op. cit., pp. 11–14.

[72]*Myths, Dreams, and Religion*, op. cit., p. 169.

[73]Joseph Campbell, *Oriental Mythology*, Vol. 2 of *The Masks of God* (New York: The Viking Press, Inc., 1962), pp. 503–504.

[74]*The Hero with a Thousand Faces*, op. cit., p. 168; Campbell notes: "See Okakura Kakuzo, *The Book of Tea* (New York: 1906). See also Daisetz Teitaro Suzuki, *Essays in Zen Buddhism* (London: 1927), and Lafcadio Hearn, *Japan* (New York: 1904)."

[75]Immanuel Kant, *Prolegomena zu einer jeden künftigen Metaphysik, die als Wissenschaft wird aufreten können*, par. 36–38.

[76]*The Inner Reaches of Outer Space*, op. cit., pp. 27–31, abr.

[77]*Myths to Live By*, op. cit., p. 23.

[78]Joseph Campbell, "Mythological Themes in Creative Literature and Art," op. cit., p. 157.

[79]Loren Eisely, *The Firmament of Time* (New York: Atheneum Publishers, 1962), p. 140; cited in *Creative Mythology*, op. cit., p. 624.

[80]*Myths to Live By*, op. cit., p. 77.

[81]Ibid., p. 97.

[82]Ibid.

[83]Joseph Campbell as quoted by Eugene Kennedy, ``Earthrise,'' in *New York Times Magazine*, April 15, 1979.

[84]Ibid.

[85]*Occidental Mythology*, op. cit., pp. 506–507; Campbell comments: "See *Primitive Mythology* (op. cit.), p. 231."

[86]*The Hero with a Thousand Faces*, op. cit., p. 156.

[87]*Myths to Live By*, op. cit., pp. 3–4.

[88]Ibid., pp. 152–153.

[89]Ibid., p. 153.

[90]Jonathan Edwards, *Sinners in the Hands of an Angry God* (Boston, 1742); cited in *The Hero with a Thousand Faces*, op. cit., pp. 127–128, abr.

[91]*The Hero with a Thousand Faces*, op. cit., p. 128.

[92]*The Gospel According to Thomas*, Coptic text, established and translated by A. Guillaumont, H.-Ch. Puech, G. Quispel, W. Till, and Yassah'abd al Masih (Leiden: E. J. Brill; New York: Harper, 1959), p. 43, Logion 77:26–27; cited in *The Inner Reaches of Outer Space*, op. cit., p. 61.

[93]James Joyce, *Ulysses* (Paris: Shakespeare and Company, 9th printing, 1927; New York: Random House, 1934), p. 38.

[94]Cited in *The Portable Jung*, op. cit., p. 634.

[95]*Meister Eckhart*, op. cit., Vol. I, *Sermons and Collations*, No. II, p. 10; cited in *Occidental Mythology*, op. cit., p. 510.

[96]Ibid.

[97]*The Hero with a Thousand Faces*, op. cit., p. 191.

[98]Joseph Campbell in Eugene Kennedy, op. cit

[99]Ibid., p. 391.

[100]*The Gospel According to Thomas*, op. cit., Logion 113:16–17, p. 57.

[101]*Occidental Mythology*, op. cit., p. 276.

[102]Ibid., p. 281.

[103]Joseph Epes Brown, *The Sacred Pipe: Black Elk's Account of the Seven Rites of the Oglala Sioux* (Norman, OK: University of Oklahoma Press, 1953), p. 4, note 2; as cited in *The Flight of the Wild Gander*, op. cit., p. 79.

[104]*The Flight of the Wild Gander*, op. cit., pp. 197–198.

[105]Editor's note in Heinrich Zimmer, *Philosophies of India*, edited by Joseph Campbell, Bollingen Series XXVI (New York: Bollingen Foundation, 1951), p. 18.

[106]*Oriental Mythology*, op. cit., p. 280.

[107]Heinrich Zimmer, *Philosophies of India*, op. cit., p. 534.

[108]*The Hero with a Thousand Faces*, op. cit., p. 160.

[109]*The Mythic Image*, op. cit., p. 419.

[110]Goethe, *Faust*, Act II, scene 5, concluding Chorus Mysticus.

[111]Joseph Campbell in Eugene Kennedy, `op. cit.

[112]*Myths to Live By*, op. cit., pp. 149–151.

[113]*The Mythic Image*, op. cit., pp. 321–322, abr.

[114]Heinrich Zimmer, "The Indian World Mother," translated by Ralph Manheim, in *The Mystic Vision, Papers from the Eranos Yearbooks*, Vol. 6, edited by Joseph Campbell, Bollingen XXX– 6 (New York: Bollingen Foundation, 1968; paperback reprint: Princeton, NJ: Princeton University Press, 1982), p. 77; originally published in *Eranos-Jahrbücher* VI (1938) by Rhein-Verlag, Zurich, Switzerland.

[115]Ibid., pp. 95–96, abr.

[116] *The Hero with a Thousand Faces*, op. cit., p. 170, note 132.

[117] James Joyce, *Finnegans Wake* (New York: Viking Press, 1939), p. 23.23–24.

[118] *The Mythic Image*, op. cit., p. 238.

[119] *The Hero with a Thousand Faces*, op. cit., p. 113.

[120] Ibid. op. cit., p. 116.

[121] See *The Mythic Image*, op. cit., pp. 327–328.

[122] Louis de la Vallée-Poussin, *Le Bouddhisme* (Paris: G. Beauchesne and Cie, 1909), p. 140; cited in *The Mythic Image*, op. cit., p. 52.

[123] *Katha Upanishad* 3.12; cited in *The Mythic Image*, op. cit., p. 52.

[124] *Vakyashudha* 13; cited in *The Mythic Image*, op. cit., p. 52.

[125] *The Mythic Image*, op. cit., p. 52.

[126] Robinson Jeffers, from "Natural Music," in *Roan Stallion, Tamar, and Other Poems* (New York: Horace Liveright, 1925), p. 232; cited in "Mythological Themes in Creative Literature and Art," op. cit., p. 175.

[127] William Blake, "The Marriage of Heaven and Hell."

[128] "Mythological Themes in Creative Literature and Art," op. cit., pp. 164–165.

[129] James Joyce, *Ulysses*, op. cit., p. 409.

[130] *The Flight of the Wild Gander,* op. cit., p. 196.

[131] Ibid., pp. 186–187.

[132] Robert Snyder, *Buckminster Fuller* (New York: St. Martin's Press, 1980), p. 100.

[133] Daisetz Teitaro Suzuki, *Essays in Zen Buddhism* (First Series), Published for the Buddhist Society, London (London, New York, Melbourne, Sydney, Cape Town: Rider and Company, n.d.), p. 58.

[134] Joseph Campbell, *The Historical Atlas of World Mythology, Volume I: The Way of the Animal Powers, Part 2: Mythologies of the Great Hunt* (New York: Harper & Row, 1988), p. xv.

[135] James Joyce, *A Portrait of the Artist as a Young Man*, op. cit., Jonathen Cape ed., p. 233; Penguin edition, p. 205.

[136] Ibid.

[137] *Mythologies of the Great Hunt*, op. cit., p. xiii.

[138]James Joyce, *A Portrait of the Artist as a Young Man*, op. cit., Penguin edition., p. 214.

[139]Ibid.; as cited in *Primitive Mythology*, op. cit., pp. 469–470.

[140]Ibid., p. 245.

[141]*Mythologies of the Great Hunt*, op. cit., p. xvii.

[142]Friedrich Nietzsche, *Die Geburt der Tragödie; oder Griechenthum und Pessimusmus* (leipzig: E. W. Fritzch, 1886), passages from the ends of Sections 1 and 16, abr. and translated by Joseph Campbell; cited in *Historical Atlas of World Mythology, Volume II: The Way of the Seeded Earth, Part 1: The Sacrifice* (New York: Harper & Row, 1988), p. 46.

[143]*Myths to Live By*, op. cit., pp. 89–90.

[144]*The Hero with a Thousand Faces*, op. cit., p. 4.

[145]Thomas Merton, "Symbolism: Communication or Communion?" in *New Directions 20* (New York: New Directions, 1968), pp. 1–2, abr.; as cited in *Myths to Live By*, op. cit., p. 265.

[146]*Myths to Live By*, op. cit., p. 91.

[147]*Chandogya Upanishad*, 3. 19. 1–3.

[148]*The Hero with a Thousand Faces*, op. cit., pp. 276–277.

[149]*Primitive Mythology*, op. cit., p. 58.

[150]Joseph Epes Brown, op. cit., pp. 3–4 and 80; cited in *The Flight of the Wild Gander*, op. cit., p. 78.

[151]*Primitive Mythology*, op. cit., p. 463.

[152]*The Hero with a Thousand Faces*, op. cit., p. 181.

[153]*Myths to Live By*, op. cit., p. 148.

[154]Erwin Schrödinger, *My View of the World,* translated by Cecily Hastings (Cambridge: Cambridge University Press, 1964), p. 95; cited in *Myths to Live By*, op. cit., p. 257.

[155]*The Flight of the Wild Gander*, op. cit., p. 197.

[156]*Myths to Live By*, op. cit., p. 257.

[157]Ibid., op. cit., p. 106.

[158]*The Gospel According to Thomas*, op. cit., Logion 3, p. 3; cited in *Mythologies of the Great Hunt*, op. cit., p. xvii.

[159]Ibid., Logion 113, pp. 55–57; as cited in *Mythologies of the Great Hunt*, op. cit., p. xviii

[160]From an anonymously edited and popularly circulated speech delivered by Chief Seattle (Seathl) in 1855; other versions have been published by Virginia Armstrong, *I Have Spoken: American History Through the Voices of the Indians* (Chicago: Sage Books, 1971); by Thomas Sanders and Walter Peck, *Literature of the American Indian* (New York: Macmillan, 1973); and in German, as Chief Seattle, *Wir sind ein Teil der Erde* (Olten und Freiburg i Brsg.: Walter-Verlag A. G. Olten, 1982); as cited in *Mythologies of the Great Hunt*, op. cit., p. 251.

[161]*Myths to Live By*, op. cit., pp. 244–245.

[162]Ibid., p. 274.

[163]Ibid., pp. 253–254.

[164]Ibid., pp. 246–247.

[165]Walt Whitman, *Leaves of Grass*, Version of the First (1855) Edition, section 48, lines 1262-1280, edited with an Introduction by Malcolm Cowley (New York: The Viking Press, 1961), pp. 82–83.

[166]*Brihadaranyaka Upanishad* 1.4.6–10, abr.

[167]*The Gospel According to Thomas*, op. cit., 99:28-30 and 95:24–28; cited in *Myths to Live By*, op. cit., pp. 258–260, abr.

[168]*Myths to Live By*, p. 263.

[169]Ibid., p. 266.

[170]Ibid., p. 275.